Just passing by
Portraits of the Third World

Just passing by

Portraits of the Third World

JON CARNEGIE

HUDSON
HAWTHORN

Published by
Hudson Publishing
6 Muir Street, Hawthorn, Victoria 3122

First published 1994

Copyright © Jon Carnegie 1994

Typeset by the publishers

Printed by Southwood Press, Marrickville, New South Wales

National Library of Australia cataloguing-in-publication data:

Carnegie, Jonathan James, 1965 – .
   Just passing by: portraits of the third world

   ISBN 0 949873 51 9

   1. Carnegie, Jonathan James, 1965- - Journeys. 2. Voyages and travels. 3. Developing countries – Description and travel. I. Title.

915.04

The author:
Jon Carnegie was born in Sydney in 1965. He was educated at Trinity Grammar School and trained as a teacher at Deakin University. He now lives in Melbourne where he teaches and works as a free-lance journalist. *Just passing by* is his first book.

Contents

Acknowledgements	6
PROLOGUE	7
ASIA	**9**
Thailand	10
Vietnam	25
Cambodia	41
India	49
Nepal	65
A STOP-OVER	
England	79
AFRICA	**83**
Egypt	84
Uganda	89
CENTRAL AMERICA	**103**
Mexico	104
El Salvador	109
Honduras	122
Nicaragua	129
Costa Rica	139
EPILOGUE	144

Acknowledgements

I would like to extend my thanks to the following people:

To Helen and Tikki Wooles, who were there at the start; to Dave Rogers and family, who have always been there; to Tony 'Cowboy' Kiers for his good humour; to Don Witt, a teacher and a gentleman; to George Blake and Margret Williams. To Harry Bell, John, Linda and Amanda Perdue, Don and Aniva Payne, the Heffer family, and Nick and Michaela Johnson, with whom I shared many Cisks and the odd 100-run partnership.

To Liz Bolton and family for their hospitality, to John, Kirsty and Ben Morrison for the Fontanella chocolate cake and to the staff and students at Verdala International School, Malta.

To Sarah and Joe Stevenson; Jane, Rachel, Michael, Diana, Angus, Charles and Jean Morrison.

To Sally Morrison because she never stops trying.

To Jo McCoy, Sue Tuckerman, Anne McCulloch, Debbie Sneddon, Tina Davis and Nick Hudson for their help in editing.

To Rohan and Leonie Brown for the pleasant Sunday mornings; to David O'Shaughnessy and Helen Reynolds for lending me their computers; to Karyne Newitt, Amanda Johnson, Chris Glass, John Hope, Jon Cash and Richard Wardrop because they have always shown an interest and finally to the staff and students at Trinity Grammar School, Kew.

I would also like to acknowledge the following who have printed extracts from this book:
> Janne Appelgren and the *Sunday Age;*
> Peter Flaherty and the Melbourne *Herald-Sun;*
> Geoff Williams and the Adelaide *Advertiser;*
> Andrew Conway and the *Sydney Morning Herald.*

*To my grandmothers,
Laura and Wendy,
both travellers in their own ways*

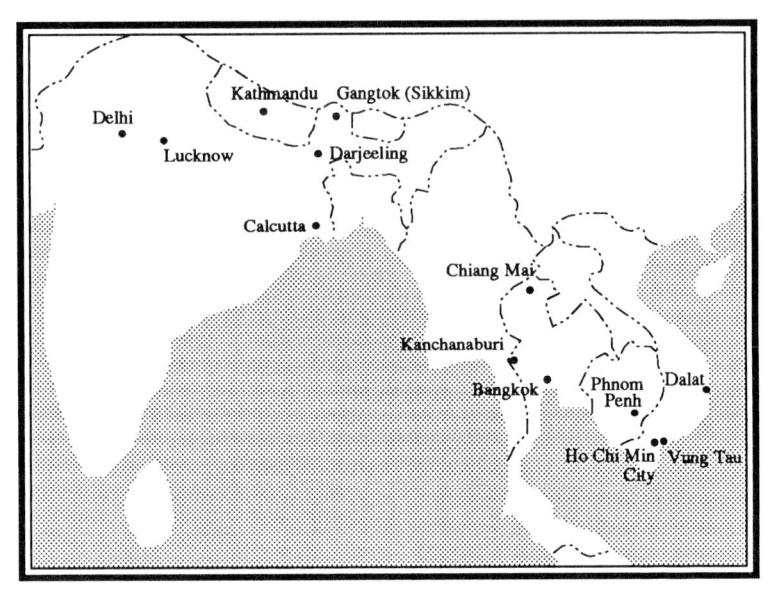

South and South-East Asia

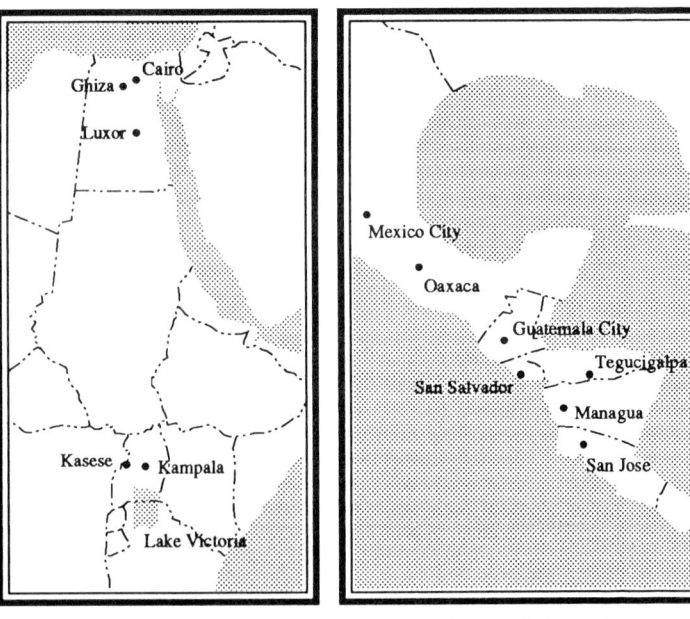

North-East Africa

Central America

Prologue

LIKE MOST AUSTRALIANS, I grew up in the suburbs. It was a leafy, happy enough existence that contained my life and all my imaginings. I was a kid who went on imaginary journeys. With my 'explorey' bag (a jungle green sack from the army surplus store) over my shoulder, I would set off most weekends into the bush or the local park under our flats. Usually I went alone, planning some separate scenario each time: lost in the bush with the Aborigines, searching for an inland sea, crossing the Simpson Desert. At school I would sit in the back row and dream of arriving in an African village full of starving people. I would live in that village and become chief, teaching the people how to grow food and survive. At other times I was a cameraman in Vietnam or Beirut, risking my life to bring the real story back home. By age seven I had crossed all the major deserts of the world, fought in all its wars and sailed all its oceans ... and I hadn't even left NSW. Real dramas were confined to small domestic problems: the dog ate the cat, the kid up the road fell off his bike, I fell off the roof collecting plums. It was a comfortable but limited existence.

In the year colour television arrived at our house, 250 000 people died in Uganda and 10 000 000 were left homeless after the floods in Bangladesh and it hardly touched my life at all. I lived in a cocoon of second-hand experiences until at twenty-three, I found myself back teaching at my old school. One by one I saw my childhood dreams slip away, until finally I wanted to chase them. That was when I decided to travel — to live in the present, to touch life.

I chose the Third World because I knew it would be different; something beyond my previous experiences. My travels through these countries were not always successful nor were they unique. If the truth be known, for most of the time I was lonely and miserable but, for perhaps one day in every month, I was higher than I had ever been before. I touched things in myself and the world that I had never known were there. These were the days that made travel worthwhile; days when I confronted my fears and prejudices and began to understand how little of the world I really knew.

This book is about capturing a few of those moments and although chronologically arranged, it is not so much a story, as a series of portraits. The events were not always comfortable and often I did not cope, but I did feel that I existed as an individual in the world and that the world had a life much larger than my own.

Looking back, my first few experiences in Thailand seem fairly pedestrian in comparison to other events in the book, but I have included them because they were real. They were a starting point; a soft entry to Asia, but one I felt I needed at the time. In hindsight, my original fears and perceptions were ridiculous, but that is what complacent middle-class living does. It teaches you to put comfortable boxes round your life; boxes that limit your access to first-hand experience. I am no great adventurer; I may never climb Everest or cross the Gobi desert, but if I have learned one thing through travel, it is that I should never be afraid to try.

ASIA

Thailand

'WHERE YOU GO? WHERE YOU GO?' taunted a skinny Thai man as I walked with feigned confidence towards the airport doors.

'I don't know,' I replied honestly.

'Come, come,' he said, smiling at me through yellowing teeth. 'I have taxi, take you Khoa San Road, many tourists, very cheap. You want girl? I am your friend, have many sister, many mother too.'

It was midnight and I had no idea where I was going to stay, so I followed the little man out of the airport.

'I'll take the taxi, but I'll leave your sisters and your mothers to themselves for a while.'

'Yes, yes, taxi Khoa San Road,' he said, ushering me into his car, which looked nothing like a taxi to me. 'Have daughter too if you like younger girl. Very good virgin every time,' he laughed, revving the taxi and turning at breakneck speed out of the car park and into mainstream traffic. Rows of daintily strung flowers swung back and forth from the rear view mirror as the driver ducked in and out of traffic breaks that weren't there, missing pedestrians, cars and bikes by centimetres. I clung grimly to the edge of my seat as he sailed through a red light, parting the oncoming swarm of moped riders in a move that Moses would have been proud of. The traffic was so heavy that I could scarcely believe it was midnight. We pulled up next to a bus that blasted carbon monoxide through a window while the mopeds closed in around us. Coughing, I turned to wind up the window only to find a moped rider's hand resting across the top of it for support. As if in acknowledgment of my distress, the taxi driver leaned forward and turned on the air-conditioner, which began to circulate chilled fumes around the car.

In the city centre, the traffic moved slowly forward against the red light, horns sounded and mopeds crept into the spaces between the cars. Not to be denied, my driver turned his steering wheel like a man possessed, and took to the footpath. We overtook the tangle and turned down a side street.

'Khoa San Road,' he announced. 'My brother have hostel here, very cheap, good girls.'

'No girls,' I replied, 'Just a room.' Then, without attempting to park, the driver got out and beckoned me to follow him into 'his brother's' hostel.

The man behind the desk was clearly not his brother but the rates seemed reasonable, so I accepted, paid the driver and assured him for the last time that I was not interested in any of the female members of his family.

The room was sparse but comfortable and after convincing the owner, too, I did not want any company for the night, I lay down exhausted.

There was a poster hanging, crooked on the back of the door. 'Welcome to Thailand', it read, 'May You Rest Here in Peace'.

KHOA SAN ROAD WAS A TRAVEL MECCA. There were tourists just like me everywhere, decking themselves out in jewelry and Thai-style clothing from the shop stands that lined the street. I had come to Thailand to get away from conformity and my own culture, only to find it was almost as firmly entrenched here as it was at home. It seemed we had all come here together to get away from each other and then recreated the very thing we were running from. I was disillusioned with myself for seeking the security of familiar-looking faces and so, on a whim, I boarded a bus and rode twenty minutes to an unknown destination.

The footpaths smelled of urine and coriander. I lost my way in a maze of tiny alleys and side streets which all looked the same: row after row of little shop stalls set up on wooden boxes with tarpaulins flapping above them. Self-consciously, I ducked under doorways and squeezed past old women cooking soup and small children selling cigarettes from cardboard trays. It was strange to be the odd one out, so big and white. I began to feel uncomfortably conspicuous.

Barefooted urchins no higher than my waist tugged at my shorts and held out hands for money. My brand-new Reeboks seemed larger and whiter than ever. I thought of taking them off and throwing them as far as I could. Instead I bought a pair of sandals; but they were too small.

An old woman perched in the gutter was stirring what looked like noodle soup in a cauldron. I stopped to watch and before I could walk away, she filled a bowl and offered it to me with a gap-toothed smile. I felt obliged to sit down as some Thais hastily procured a seat for me and gathered around in anticipation. Neither the aroma nor the texture gave me any indication of the origin of the broth and so, lifting the bowl carefully to my mouth, I took my first taste. It was salty but quite drinkable and, smiling politely between sips, I managed to finish only to discover at the bottom of the bowl was a chicken's head, its beak partially open and an eyeless socket staring up at me. I thanked everyone and fumbled through my guide book to find the phrase for 'how much?' Using my fingers and some terribly pronounced Thai, I tried to get the message across. The shopkeeper laughed.

'It's 10 baht,' she said, scooping the chicken's head out of my bowl and tossing it back into her pot.

'You speak English!'

'You bet, very best English.' she said. 'Where you come from?'

'Australia,' I replied.

'Ah,' she said. 'Australia, Sydney; kangaroo, very big.'

PAT-PONG ROAD was teaming with westerners crawling like ants over an open sore. It's the fascination and promised satisfaction of picking the scab that sells. Years of social conditioning were being put to the test; uncontrolled gluttony was everywhere, Western roles were reversed; fat ugly men became sex symbols, poor men became rich. Suddenly titillating dreams were accessible and morality expendable.

At the flood lit street stalls that lined the avenue, businessmen stocked up on fake Chanel perfume for their wives, and holiday-makers on a budget stuffed their bags full of 'Rolexes', like children let loose in a lolly store. Fat, pink Germans strolled hand-in-hand with sylph-like Thai girls, their giant sausage fingers glowing medium-rare on the dark-skinned limbs. The girls smiled uncomfortably and then swore eternal love.

I loitered outside a number of bars, anonymous in the crowd, unsure whether or not I wanted go inside. Lights flashed and Thai spruikers yelled from doorways, darting their arms out like eels grabbing at passers-by. 'Good show, good show, live tricks.' The bars were all the same but despite the fact that no one cared, I wanted to make it clear I was only here to look, so I postponed going into one as long as possible. Eventually I chose 'Girlie Alive'.

The empty entrance hall flashed with lights and mirrors. Music pulsed from behind the doors; a man came out and we passed on the stairs without looking at each other.

Inside was noisy, dark and crowded. Six girls were dancing topless on stage. Self-consciously, I sat down next to a group of tourists, surrounded by bar girls dressed only in little yellow G-stings. One of them moved over and sat next to me. I looked at her and hunted for something to say. In the end the best I could do was, 'Hello, my name is Jon.'

On the table next to me one of the girls ran her hand across a tourist's chest, and looked at him from the corner of her eyes.

'You love me?' she asked. 'You want marry me?'

Apparently disconcerted by seduction without all the preliminaries, the man did not know what to say.

'No, no,' he replied. 'I'm just here for a drink.'

She did not understand.

'You hold me now,' she said.

Awkwardly he placed an arm around her, like a boy carrying a water balloon, afraid it would break.

Embarrassed, I reached for my drink. The cultural contradiction was hard to explain. No one looked on disapprovingly as men walked in and out of the back rooms with the girls. In fact, if anything, the normally placid, modest Thais seemed to encourage it.

I reached again for my drink. What else could I do? The girl beside me put her hand on my leg. Embarrassed, I lifted it away and began to tap the musical beat with my fingers.

'Why you take my hand away?' she asked, seemingly offended. 'You no like it?'

Inadequately, I mumbled something about degradation, exploitation and cross-cultural understanding. My socialised Western responses and defences were suddenly and alarmingly inappropriate. I was no longer in control, I was no longer doing the manipulation; she was and I was a child again.

On the stage in front of us the women danced seductively with each other, much to the delight of some drunken Germans who clapped enthusiastically with each new movement.

Why am I staring? I thought. The music blared, 'Strip for me and I'll strip for you,' ran the lyrics.

A waitress saw my empty glass.

'You want food, drink, sex?' she asked. There was a category for each on the bill.

'I'll have a Coke, please,' I replied. The girl by my side looked up sharply.

'You no love me?' she protested.

'Make that two Cokes,' I added. The girl smiled and placed her arm around my shoulder.

A woman emerged from backstage, wearing nothing but a tiny skirt. Her face was expressionless. Few of the men bothered to look up, they were too busy trying to talk to the girls on their laps. She stood before us and reaching beneath her skirt she proceeded to pull out a string of razor blades, tied one to the other by a piece of twine. In shock I peered forward to see if they were real; but after all, what difference did it make?

'What's your name?' I asked the girl by my side, driven by some instinct to divert her attention from the stage.

'I am 61,' she replied, pointing proudly to the numbered badge she wore pinned to the side of her G-string. 'You want marry me? Me very cheap, very good. We live in America?'

She looked like a five-year-old girl asking for an ice-cream. I felt like a fifty-year-old man offering her one.

It was difficult to keep things in perspective. I had come to Bangkok to find a different world but now that it was in front of me, I did not know what to do with it. Twenty-four hours had shattered twenty-four years of Western socialisation – perhaps we are only as moral as our circumstances permit us to be. Within five minutes I felt as if I ought to have experienced every emotion from desire to disgust and back again but all I could feel was confused.

The popular perception – that the West was exploiting the East – was an illusion. Here in the bar, 'for a bit of harmless fun', there was everyone from the German lawyer to the American businessman, gripping tightly to conservative, Western convention with one hand, while softly stroking the backside of promiscuity with the other, disorientated in a whirlpool of lust and logic, unable to differentiate between the two. Lights flashed, women danced and every defence they put up failed, was eroded in varying degrees by Bangkok's subtle, subservient manipulation.

Opposite me was a fat-faced Australian with a beautifully compact, dark-skinned Thai girl perched like a butterfly on his knee. She smiled in his face, whispered into his ear; and laid one hand softly on his leg and the other around his back and onto his wallet. I had to laugh. My morality ceased to have meaning in this environment. I was face to face with a dark side of western morality. 'Go on,' it said. 'Let passion rule, participate, encourage.'

Instead I stood up to leave. The girls at the next table laughed. They seemed happy enough, and had I not looked across the room to the corner, that might have been my last impression of the Bangkok bar. On the stairs that led to the back rooms, a girl sat, huddled over, her head resting sideways on her knees. She was crying, her mascara running in black lines down her face. Without the make-up she looked about fourteen. I ceased to see the situation and started to see the people. The daughters of hill tribe families taken from their homes; Bangkok street kids with no other option; young girls, who back in Australia would still have been studying at school.

Not two days ago I had been walking the quiet suburban streets of Melbourne. Tonight, in a Bangkok bar, the girl next to me would have married me for $25. As I turned to leave, she grabbed my sleeve and handed me a cardboard drinks coaster from the table. On one side it read 'Girlie Alive Bar, Open 24 hours'. On the other, she had written four simple words: 'Jon, I love you', and signed them '61'.

THE FRONT OF THE BUS bound for Mae Hong Son was so covered in Coke stickers and hanging Buddhas that the driver could hardly see where he was going. The rear vision mirror was shrouded in flowers and on the video player two kickboxers were laying into each other, while a bunch of Americans cheered loudly in the back of the bus. We drove all night in a perpetual traffic jam, the driver periodically banging on the dash with a wrench, trying to get the air-conditioner to work. When it finally started, the air was so cold and strong that I had to remove the head-rest from my seat and wear it like a hat, to stop getting a headache.

We drove all night, stopping and starting, overtaking at breakneck speeds and then waiting for hours at overcrowded road houses while the driver ate and slept. At the bus stations, hawkers tried to sell us strings of flowers, Tiger Balm and cigarettes. Others banged on the side of the bus as we pulled in offering fruit and soft drinks in plastic bags with crushed ice. The lights of passing vehicles flashed in through the windows, car horns blared and breaks screeched and I began to wish I'd chosen to fly.

Saturated by the tourist trade, the cultural and environmental heritage of Mae Hong Son was little more than a watered-down memento of the past. Idealistically, I had envisaged a remote jungle village, untouched by Westerners. Instead I found travellers were everywhere, people just like me. I could not get away from myself. Treks were sold like used cars, with all the extras thrown in. Hundreds of signs with many variations of spelling boasted the most action-packed one or two-day treks. *'Breakfast in Lisu village, lunch with red Karen Indians, dinner with white Karen. Cross border into Burma spend night with real rebels (with guns), smoke dope with village elder, cross poppy fields, take elephant trek and free raft ride for six dollars.'* The cultural exchange was not what I had anticipated. Coca-colonisation, as it has become known, was everywhere and the more Westerners tried to run away from it, the more they were confronted with it despite themselves. The Thais in their cunningness had cashed in.

My friend Tony (who had joined me from Australia for two weeks) and I decided upon two local guides recommended by the manager of our hostel and met them at six the next morning. The older man, Swing, wore fake Levi's and plastic shoes. 'Good for trekking', he said, pointing with farcical confidence to the ridged soles. His offsider, 'Junior', who was busy loading bananas into his Mickey Mouse back-pack, had little to say. It appeared he was learning the trade.

In the still of the early morning we left the village and followed a track into the jungle. We hardly spoke as Swing and Junior walked ahead along a well-worn path where I had naively expected we would be cutting our way through virgin rain forest with machetes. Lolly wrappers littered the trail, across the valley, bald hilltops protruded like over-sized ant-hills where the trees had been logged leaving huge ugly scars. We didn't know where we were going, only that we were heading for Burma.

I tried to hide my disappointment by using the scars to reconstruct what it must have been like to walk through before the Westerners had arrived in their droves. I envied the great explorers and I respected their courage but the childish 'Biggles-like' notion that they came with good intentions and then left the places they discovered untouched was rapidly disappearing. European explorers may have travelled into the unknown, but they carried Europe in their heads. They discovered themselves as masters over distance and ancient peoples and indoctrinated them in the ways of the west, forcing an unworkable union, from which the likes of Mae Hong Son have emerged like the bastard children, cobbling a cultural niche between two worlds.

An hour into the trip it began to rain, huge drops, falling like silver daggers for about fifteen minutes. The track became muddy and water ran in trickles down my spine. I watched the steam rise from Tony's back as he trudged a few paces ahead. I enjoyed walking in the rain, a mixture of sweat and water dripping down my face, the rain drumming in my ears

At our first river crossing the rain stopped. Swing and Junior waited as we negotiated the log bridge over the water, watched by the buffalos lazing downstream. Motionless, they stared, occasionally exhaling through flared nostrils. Swing laughed. 'Photo, photo,' he cried pointing proudly at the lolling beasts.

Further downstream we came across a man lashing bamboo poles together. The conquered strike back, I thought. Years ago he may have made rafts to carry the locals and their goods between villages. Today they carried tourists and he charged twice as much. We bought a raft from him, loaded our packs on it and headed down river. There was no getting away from the fact that he had made hundreds of such rafts for tourists and that we were no one special, but it was fun.

Towards evening we came to a small village where children with runny noses raced to greet us. They held out grubby hands for money and offered to sell us Cokes and carry our packs.

'Karen Indians,' said Swing. 'Rebel tribe, very proud.'

The euphemism lingered as we wandered through the village. American rap songs blasted from the doorways of grass huts. For 10 baht children would smile, and look happy or sad for a photograph. For an extra 10 they'd throw on their traditional costumes over their Michael Jackson T-shirts. I was sick of the facade and even sicker in the knowledge that it was tourists like me who had created it.

At dusk, Tony and I decided to go for a stroll in the jungle. From above the village, we watched as the locals rushed from their grass huts to greet another group of tourists arriving by raft. It cracked us up and we continued into the jungle where the track began to descend steeply into a clearing until we heard a voice and a man in army greens stepped from the bushes, blocking our way. His jaw was set and he stared at us, gripping a pistol in his right hand. No one moved. I ceased to be a spectator, I was me, firmly inside myself and the world appeared very small. The man grunted, gesturing for us to leave and we turned, walking quickly until we were out of sight and then, simultaneously, sprinting back to the village.

I lay awake for hours that night, frustrated at my reactions to the incident on the track. Here was I, in the Third World, seeking my great adventure, and discovering that, as soon as I stood face to face with it, my immediate reaction was to turn and run back to safety; back to the things I knew. I looked across at Tony, the usually hard lines of his face relaxed in sleep. For him this was just a holiday, from which he would be going home soon, but for me it was supposed to be a total release from my past. I had given up the security of the things I had worked towards for many years: my job, my girlfriend, my home, the things I had thought would bring me satisfaction. I had gone out into the world alone, expecting to find adventure but so far had only found the seemingly unbreakable bonds of my past.

The following day we found ourselves ridiculously perched behind the ears of a large grey elephant as it crashed out of control along the jungle track. Branches flicked into my face and my legs chafed against the roughness of the elephant's hide as it followed Swing and Junior to our lunch stop. I'd long since given up any hope of ever crossing into Burma and all I wanted now was for the trek to end.

At lunch Swing complied with my wish by producing a pistol from his backpack. Tony and I looked on in apprehension as he fired a round into a nearby tree. It occurred to me that Swing could easily turn around and shoot us.

Instead he unloaded the cartridge, turned politely to us and said, 'Trek is over now. You can go.' He held the gun up and waved us on. 'Follow this trail,' he continued. 'It will lead you back to the village.'

'But I thought we were in Burma,' I stammered. Swing laughed but he did not answer.

Stunned, we picked up our packs. I was glad of Tony's company. He had a sense of the absurd which helped in situations like this. We started back to the village, eating jelly-babies and laughing in a mixture of apprehension and relief as we went. It took all afternoon.

When we arrived back it was nearly sunset and the evening air had taken the edge off the day's heat. I left Tony at the hostel and continued walking, wanting to have some time alone and to recapture my thoughts. I relaxed and listened to the sounds of my feet walking, my scalp and face stinging from the day's sun. I allowed my imagination to drift and my body to unwind.

Strains of a familiar song began to reach my ears but I couldn't quite work out what it was. I followed the hollow crackle and came on a house in a clearing. Just inside the door there was an old gramophone on a wooden table. Frank Sinatra filled the still air.

> *Oh I'd like to climb a mountain,*
> *and reach the highest peak,*
> *but it doesn't thrill me half as much*
> *as dancing cheek to cheek.*

A barefooted, red-haired man sat nearby in a wicker chair, the smoke from his cigarette bleeding its way between his fingers and curling up the length of his arm. His face was caught in a dying ray of sunlight as he rested his outstretched arm along the balcony railing.

'Hello,' I said.

The man looked up. 'Good evening,' he replied in an Irish accent.

'We're still open if you'd like to have a look.' He gestured with a backwards nod towards the door.

It hadn't occurred to me that the house doubled as a shop. I thanked him and went in. The interior was large and square with folding screens which opened up two of the four walls, to create a veranda effect. The stained-wood floor matched the parallel rafters running across the roof. The side wall was covered in shelving, full of English-language books stacked in alphabetical order with white price tags stuck to the spines.

It was about six o'clock, and the setting sun fanned through the cracks in the roof, casting shadows on the veranda outside. A slight breeze blew off the Pai River and palm leaves bobbed like little string puppets, causing sun spots to dance on the floor.

From where I stood I could see through the back of the house into the palm jungle behind. At a desk in the back corner, a young Thai woman sat quietly behind a stack of books, covering them individually with plastic. She was slight and dark. I watched her work: unobtrusive and dexterous. Her bobbed black hair fanned in even lines across the side of her face as she bent forward. She worked, uninhibited by my presence. The nonchalant confidence in her movements made me think that perhaps she and the man outside were lovers.

I passed my eye along the row of familiar titles, picked one at random and began to read.

'We sell mostly classics,' the man said from outside.

'Oh, you have a nice collection. How much is this one?' I asked, holding up a Hermann Hesse novelette.

'Twenty-five baht,' replied the man. 'Would you like a cup of tea?'

I accepted and paid for the book.

We sat at a table in the middle of the shop and the man introduced himself as Richard. The girl was his wife. Her name was Son Kit.

'She owns the place,' he said. 'Foreigners aren't allowed to own land on their own in Thailand.'

An hour passed while we sipped tea and talked. Richard was an Irishman who had come to Thailand from Ireland ten years earlier on holiday. He had met and married Son Kit almost at once and they lived, Thai style, in the loft above the shop.

'Don't you get bored out here alone?' I asked.

'I'm not alone,' he replied. 'My wife is with me.'

I was a little embarrassed at the naivety of my question and tried to change tack.

'Do many foreigners come here to buy?'

'A few like yourself stumble across us now and then. We sell enough to get by.'

The bamboo popped in the neighbouring farm while birds wove their songs through the air. A dog lounged in the shade of a motor scooter on the front lawn. Monks tolled their bells from the monastery above the village, to signal prayer time. In the distance, the Mekong Hills.

I thought of the day; all I had set out to achieve and where I had ended up. I was envious of Richard, finding his niche, creating his own life, content to live in the present. Laughing to myself, I thanked him for the tea and, as I headed towards the door, I asked him if he had any plans to advertise the business in the village.

'Christ, no,' he replied, looking at me as though I was strange. 'It might attract more people.'

THE TRIP FROM BANGKOK to Kanchanaburi took two hours. We travelled on a first class bus, full of Japanese on a package holiday. They chatted in their little white hats and took photos through the bus windows of just about everything we passed.

When I arrived I booked in at a guesthouse on the banks of the River Kwai, dumped my pack, padlocked the door and went to hire a bike.

As a schoolboy I had been uninspired by history from books. On hot, sunny days, I'd gaze at the huge gum tree near the window of my classroom while World War II and the courts of Henry VIII were just noises in the background.

For me, the history of World War II had always been in my grandmother's face. She could speak fondly of a time when Australians and their families were united in a common cause; and also extremely bitterly, when she remembered the death of her brother in Alexandria and of her fiance in Lebanon. She was of a generation who felt things, rather than intellectualised them. To her, war did not have rational solutions, only emotional outcomes. History books could not capture the tears that welled in her eyes when she talked of the war. She had a dignity that came not from any great knowledge or understanding, but from her access to raw emotion.

Between June 1942 and October 1943 over 15 000 Australian POWs were forced to work on the Burma railway. Along with other Allied troops, it was estimated that by the time the railway was completed, one man had lost his life for every sleeper laid on the 415 kilometre track.

The town of Kanchanaburi, on the Thai end of the railway, has two war cemeteries which together contain more than seven thousand individual graves.

It was already late afternoon when I arrived and the Thai guard sleeping on the street outside the gate did not notice as I slipped past. I was immediately struck by the neatness of the place; flowers in clipped beds, the grass short and uncommonly green, the gravestones in rows like soldiers on parade.

As I moved between the rows, I was overcome by a strange feeling of security; a feeling I had felt years before when on a trip to the War Memorial in Canberra with my grandmother. She had refused to go in, saying she'd wait outside until I'd finished. Climbing up the stone steps and past the honour boards inside the doors, I can remember feeling invincible. Everything was so big and solid, the roof so high. I wandered alone, surrounded by the echoes of imaginary armies, touching brass statues, captivated by model soldiers who gazed at me proudly, like the smiling faces in the sepia prints sent home from the Front. Legends were intact, flags flew and I had wondered why my grandmother could not come inside.

The Kanchanaburi tombstone engravings painted vivid pictures of boys playing kick-to-kick in suburban streets, of young city men awkwardly courting their girlfriends in Melbourne's Botanical Gardens, of farmers' sons rising at dawn to milk the cows in Gippsland. They were everywhere, secure and solid under their concrete blocks, as in my childhood memories of the Canberra War Memorial. Meanwhile, somewhere back home, their faded photos looked down from the mantelpieces in the living rooms, a fragment of an Australia now passing into history.

> 5821941 Lance Corp.
> D. L. Jeffery; Suffolk Reg.
> Age 23
> I often think of you my son,
> and wonder why you had to die.
> Love forever Mum.

> 6082194 Serg. A. W. Clarke; Highland Gunners
> Age 26
> From your wife and the son who you never met
> but who will always remember you.
> Rest in Peace dear.
> Love Annie & Andrew Jnr.

> M. N. Moulton
> 135 3427 Corp.
> Australian Armed Forces
> Loved Son of
> Mr & Mrs P. H. Moulton
> Korrumburra, Victoria, Australia.
> 'R. I. P. Son'
> 28th April 1944 Age 21

The parents are old or dead now, the children grown, but for every one of them, there is a moment every year or so, when something reminds them of the past; not of legends in War Memorials, but of vulnerable, all-too-destructable brothers, sons, husbands and friends.

Birds chirped in the trees. On the street outside a man riding on his bicycle looked inquisitively over the fence, and the cemetery guard, frail and old, continued to sleep, propped up in the shade by the marble pillar of the entrance gate.

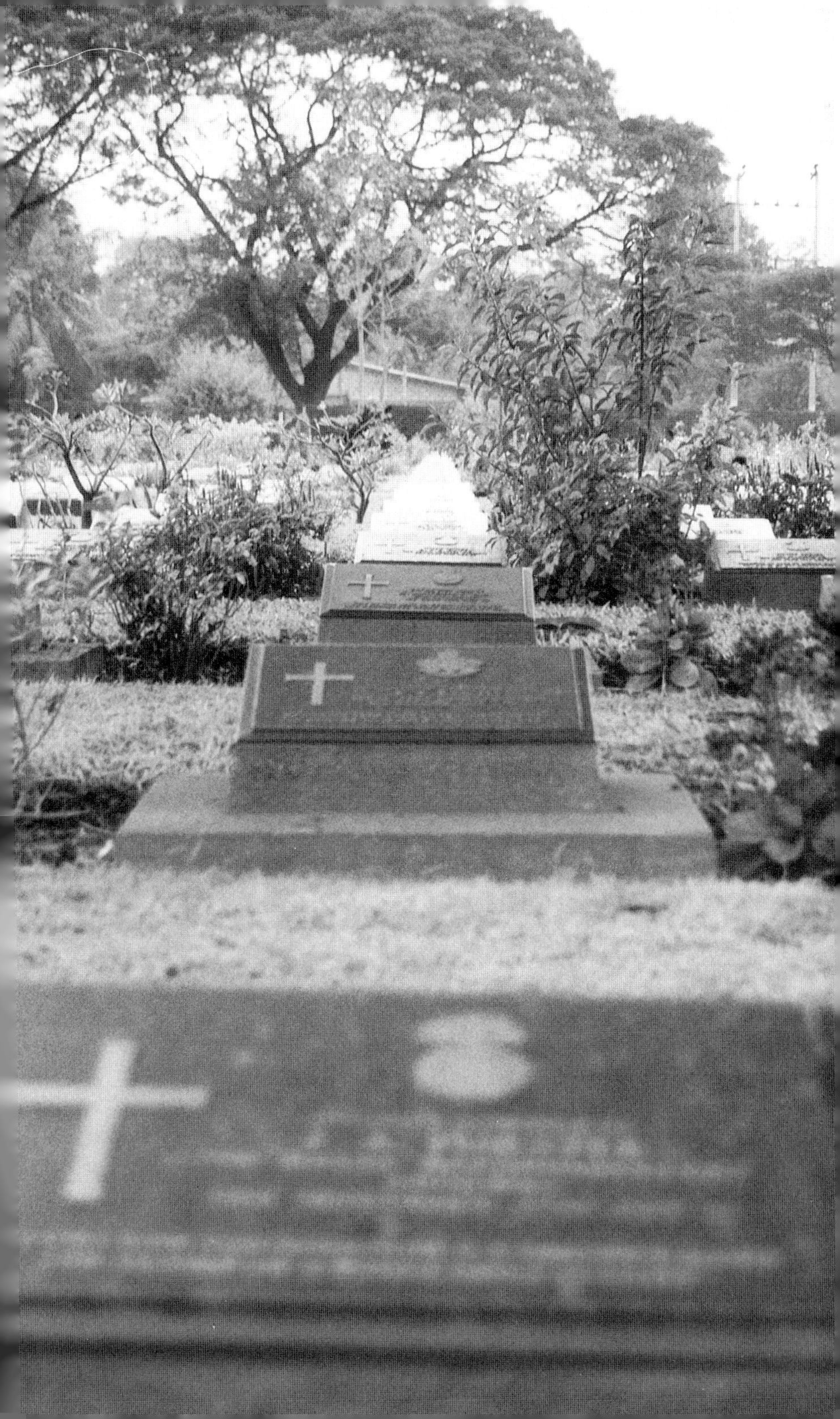

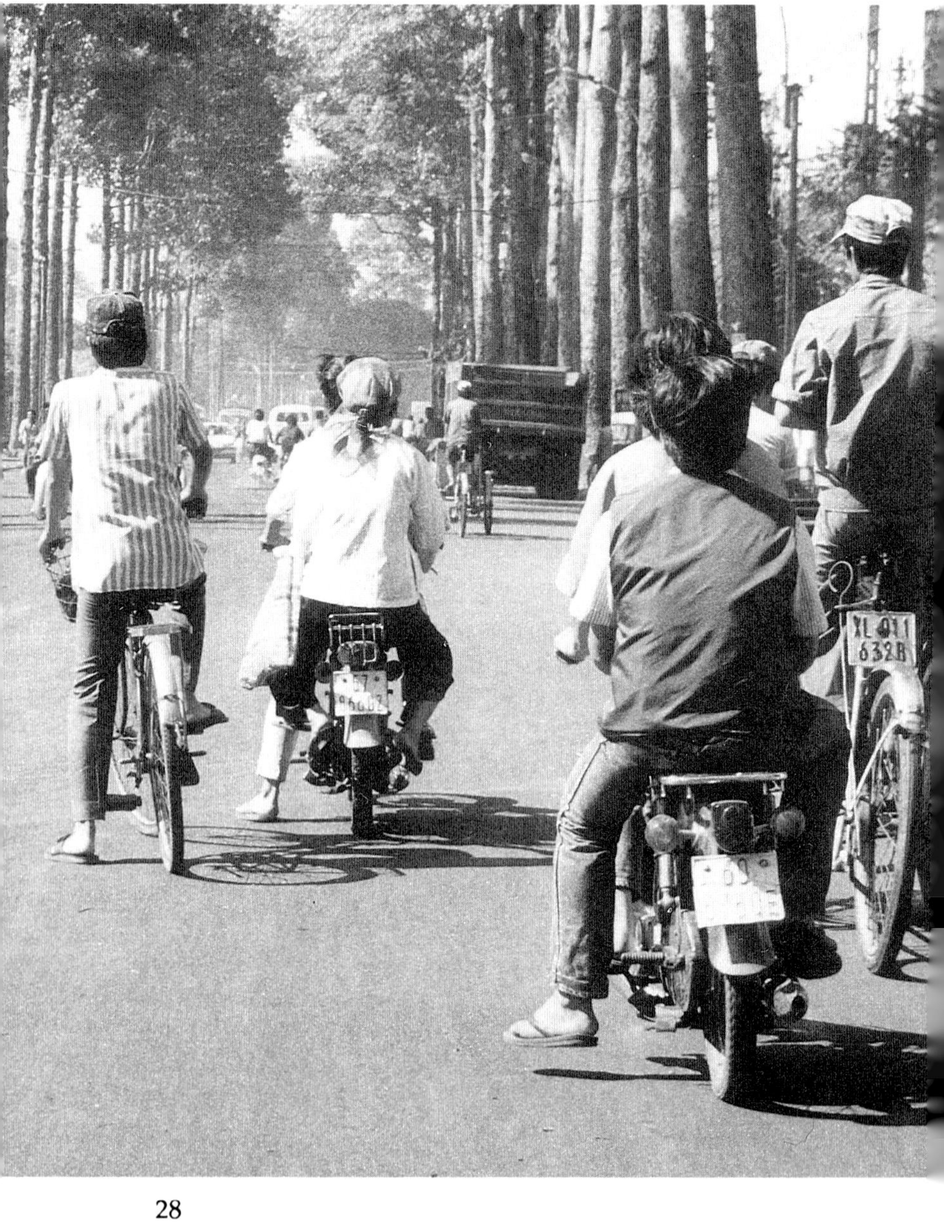

Vietnam

AIR VIETNAM FLIGHT 851 began to taxi before the doors were closed. Children played in the aisles and overhead luggage compartments sprang open with each jolt the plane made. My belt buckle wouldn't fasten so I tied it in a knot and mentally rehearsed the various crash poses I could remember being instructed in on other flights. There was a piece of rope dangling above my head, with the words, 'In Case Of Emergency Pull On String' written below it. Considering having no seat belt an emergency, I pulled and the string came away in my hand.

Not so many years ago Ton Son Nhut was the busiest airport in the world. They say that in 1970 flying in was like passing over an ant hill through which a child had just dragged a stick. Today, however, it was deserted. My first impression of Vietnam was of emptiness: row upon row of blackened hangars lined the runway; in the pit yard further on lay abandoned planes, their wings bobbing slightly in the wind, their smashed canopies now homes for spiders.

For me, Vietnam had only ever been a war in the background of my childhood. I can remember sitting in our lounge room in the early '70s with a group of Mum's university friends. After a heated argument about the war, we were watching a TV news reporter interview injured soldiers returning home; one had had terrible burn marks on his face. It had shocked me to see the war so close. Until then it had always been this thing being televised for us overseas. I think the others felt the same too, because as the news continued the atmosphere in the room changed. Antagonism drifted away. Peg's boyfriend, who had yelled the loudest during the argument, shifted uncomfortably in his chair and the echoes of his ranting hung heavily in the air. We saw the things that were real; things that transcended philosophy and crushed the postwar generation of the '60s. I curled up on my mother's lap and she stroked my hair, the way parents do when they want to soothe you. Nobody spoke.

AT CUSTOMS no one seemed to have a hat that fitted. Short men called out and gestured to even shorter women, who processed multiple-entry visas and shuffled people to luggage collection.

'Ookdaloi?' inquired a middle-aged woman as she stamped my passport.

'Pardon?' I replied.

'Ookdaloi,' she repeated. 'Cheap Charlie. You go down there through gate three,' and she laughed melodiously.

The car park was full of Peugeots. A petite woman dressed in a silk *ao dai* stepped forward. She touched her hands gently together under her chin and bowed slightly, her bobbed hair fanning across her face as Son Kit's had done in the Thai book shop.

'Parlez-vous Français, Monsieur?'

'Non, je ne parle pas. Je suis Ookdaloi,' I said, remembering the woman at Customs. She, too, laughed and gestured towards the car.

It was hard to imagine that just two years ago, due to government restrictions, there were virtually no cars on these streets. Now they drove, mostly down the middle of the road, spreading the swarms of cyclists as they went. The only rule here, it seemed, was: don't get hit. Like thousands of black tennis balls floating down a rapid river, heads bobbed along above their bicycles, merging into mainstream traffic wherever space permitted and often where it didn't.

Transport was at a premium in Ho Chi Minh City. Whole families rode on single motor scooters. Young children peered from boxes on the backs of bicycles. Old men on pushbikes laden two metres high with all kinds of merchandise weaved in and out around us. Turning riders gesticulated with an elaborate array of hand signals, as if conducting the symphony of horns which blared out in protest as the cyclists cut centimetres in front of oncoming traffic and darted into side streets. And through it all, unflustered, untouched by the fumes and the bustle, the beautiful white-silk-clad women rode, gliding like giant swans.

I dined that night with my guide Nga at the top floor Palais Hotel restaurant. In the background a duet played a melancholy version of Paul McCartney's *Yesterday*, while French-style Vietnamese waiters took our orders. Through the window Ho Chi Minh City was still bustling. In the town square below, we watched in silence as the faded face of Ho Chi Minh smiled over his city, lit up in consecutive stills by the flashing lights of the Palais dance hall.

In truth, Ho Chi Minh City was nothing like I expected. Each morning as Nga and I left the hotel we were swamped by trishaw drivers, wanting to give us tours. They had seen I carried American dollars. Green was gold in Vietnam, and they wanted it. University students stopped me in the streets, begging us to send them US textbooks. Fat American businessmen sat in hotels and smoked cigars, laying the groundwork for the day the US lifted its embargoes on Vietnam. Communism was splitting at the seams and the strain on a nation that had fought so hard to establish it was beginning to show. Run-down monuments dotted the streets; the former American embassy, once the showpiece of Vietnamese ingenuity and dedication, was now a crumbling communications centre.

At the sides of the streets, rows of skinny legs dangled over the sides of countless trishaws. Behind them, legless beggars moved on hand-held blocks of wood. The streets were cracked, and the footpaths dirty. Most of the beggars and trishaw drivers had been former South Vietnamese soldiers, many of them professionals, forbidden by the Government to work after the war. Most had spent at least seven years in re-education camps. They survived now by hustling both foreigners and locals alike.

'Where you go sir? Where you come from? Oh, Australia! Ookdaloi, number one. Please sit, sir. You pay US, okay?'

Ironically for these men, abandoned by the Americans in 1975, they now relied on the language they had learned during the war and the US dollars they traded on the black market.

The black market itself was very extensive. Here, in a country where people lived crowded on boats because they couldn't afford houses, where milk comes powdered and dress fashion hasn't changed in more than a thousand years, you could buy anything you liked, from crocodile skin golf bags to fully operational US or Russian machine-guns.

The black-market area was downtown. The streets were filled with vendors selling clothes. Most of them worked in factories where the managers did not pay in cash, but instead allowed the workers to take a pile of clothes each week.

We walked the streets for about thirty minutes until we reached a doorway. A short, fat, Chinese man of about fifty emerged jovially from behind a curtain at the back of the dimly lit shop. He greeted Nga warmly.

'This is Mr Lac Long, the king of the black market,' she said. 'Anything you want, you speak to him.'

Lac Long stepped forward.

'And what may I do for you, sir?' he inquired, proudly grasping the lapels of his jacket and rocking himself on the balls of his feet. 'Russian caviar? French champagne?'

The shop walls were laden with everything under the sun: elephant-foot doorstops, whole leopard skins, dusty bottles of imported wines, hats, coats, diamonds and gold were displayed haphazardly on racks and in dusty cabinets.

'Tickets to the World Series perhaps. Or maybe the Bolshoi?'

'Got any Vegemite?' I asked, hoping to catch him out.

'Certainly sir,' he replied with satisfaction as he reached into a small cupboard behind several pairs of Mickey Mouse ears. 'Small or large jar?'

Lac Long then took us into his back room.

'I once sold a helicopter,' he said, almost incidentally as he took a drawer containing hundreds of hat pins, medals, and other war relics from a shelf and gave me a couple.

'Where on Earth do you get all this stuff?' I asked.

'Where does one get anything in Vietnam?' Lac Long smiled as he escorted us to the door. 'On the black market of course.'

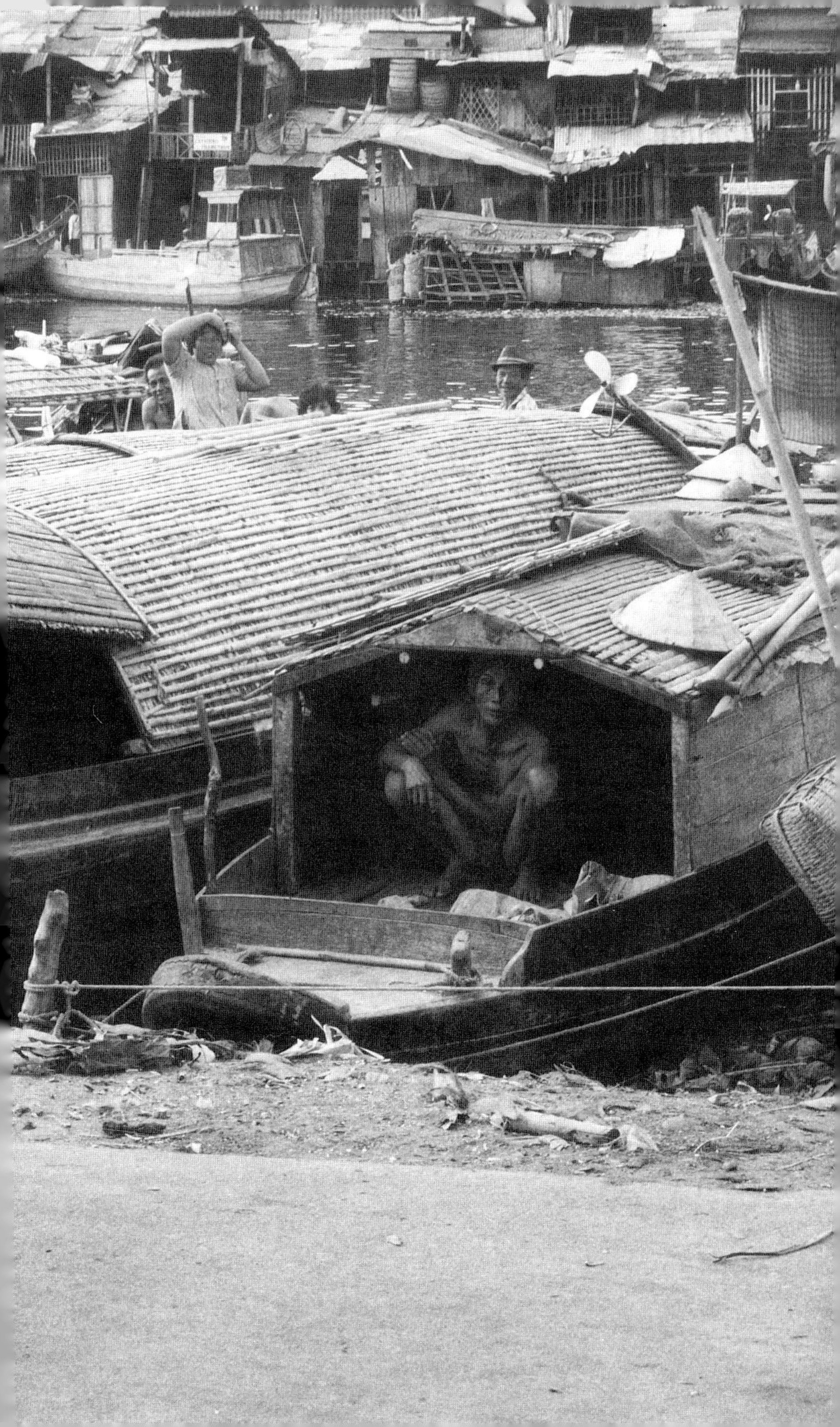

I spent my final night in Ho Chi Minh City on the top floor of the Rex Hotel listening to a large American businessman while he smoked and hypothesised about the future of Vietnam. 'American dollars speak all languages in Vietnam now' he said gesturing in a proud arc with his cigar. 'Even the beggars won't accept anything else.' he laughed. 'In five years there'll be more Americans here than in Hawaii. Communism's on its knees – the South Vietnamese are just waiting, thread in hand, to sew on the patches when it finally keels over. Kinda makes you wonder who won the war, don't it ?' he chuckled.

WE WERE ARRESTED on the way to Long Tan. My friends Philip and Albie, whom I had met at the hotel, were taking me to see the site of the famous Australian battle, but unfortunately we were not carrying the correct travel documentation.

We had stopped at an old church where Australian soldiers had hidden during the battle. Albie, who was an Australian veteran, was filming the sites for his mates, while Philip and I looked on. As usual, villagers had gathered to watch. We had been there about fifteen minutes when a young man emerged from the crowd pointing a machine-gun at us. Albie stopped filming, I froze. Philip's driver, Joseph, asked him what the problem was and we were told that we could not film without the permission of the town committee.

We were escorted under guard to a long, wooden building, where Albie, Joseph and Philip were taken inside for questioning. I was told to stay in the car. While I waited, my captor kept his machine-gun trained on me. It is strange to be so close to death. At no stage did I fear that the boy would actually pull the trigger, and yet the thought that a single contraction of his finger would end my life was bizarre, almost surreal. I could think of nothing else to do, so I smiled at him. The villagers, all laughed. It broke the tension and the boy smiled back and challenged me to an arm wrestle; which, needless to say, he won.

It took Albie two hours to explain, through Joseph, that we meant no harm and that we had come in peace to Long Tan, but when he eventually returned and we were allowed to go, he was pleased that he had been able to communicate with the committee. I was worried by the thought that some of the men on the committee had lost family or friends during the fighting there and wouldn't take kindly to our presence; but nothing could have been further from the truth. The villagers bade us goodbye. I waved, winking to my captor, who waved back and then, trailing his gun like a toddler's teddy bear, disappeared into the crowd.

I spent a large amount of time in Vietnam searching for traces of the Australian involvement in the war; Long Tan where seventeen Australians had been killed; Nui Dat; the Baria theatre, the fishing village of Vung Tau; names that are hardly known at all by most Australians but firmly entrenched in the minds of those who served there.

Sadly I found nothing but dusty, deserted, plains miles from nowhere. There was nothing to show for the loss of life; for the hollow political rhetoric that had sent conscripts to fight; no Anzac legend, no plaques or memorials; just a few fifty- or sixty-year-old villagers, who would occasionally recognise my accent, look up and nod, 'Ookdaloi, G'day cobber.'

HE WAS A BEAUTIFUL LITTLE BOY with straight dark hair and wide, excited eyes that seemed blissfully unaware of the complexities of life. The streets of Vung Tau were his home; he had known nothing else and he slept on a mat in the tall grass behind my hotel fence. His only possessions were the clothes he wore and a silver cross his father had given him which he hung around his neck.

The hotel doorman told me the boy's parents had died in Ho Chi Minh City when he was five. After their deaths, he and a friend had stowed away in the luggage compartment of a bus bound for Vung Tau.

Had he stayed in Ho Chi Minh City, he could have gone to a government orphanage and learned to pick rice for 25 cents a day. He was, I thought, better off in Vung Tau. Here he had joined one of the street gangs run by the trishaw drivers, who had taught him to beg and steal. His spoils were turned over to the driver, in return for protection and just enough money for food.

Our first contact came when I was having lunch with some Vietnamese friends from the hotel. The boy appeared from nowhere and sat down with us. There was something charming in his boldness, which set him apart from the other street kids who worked the same area. He, like so many of Vietnam's young, appeared Amerasian, his beaming smile and wide brown eyes, full of confidence.

'You number one Ookdaloi,' he said, hugging my biceps and leaning his head against my shoulder. My friends laughed and listened while the boy rabbited on in Vietnamese as if he had known us for ever.

'He says you're the number one Australian,' said my friend. 'He says you watch him from the balcony of the big hotel.'

Despite warnings from my friends that Quan was only trying to rip me off, I trusted him. He was not pushy for money or food. He bore the signs of one who has spent time on the streets; the soles of his feet were cracked and hard, and his hands, although small and delicate, were as calloused as a labourer's. Constant exposure to the sun had tanned his already dark skin.

He shared my meal. It was a pleasure to provide for him and yet I was intimidated, for, unlike Western children, Quan did not need an adult to survive. I was simply a means of obtaining those things he had been getting by himself, every day of his life since he was five.

Our friendship grew. Quan would wait for me at the bottom of the hotel steps and we would walk to the beach where he showered. It was strange to follow him, so young, through the back alleys of Vietnam. I placed myself completely in his care but, at the first sign of danger, such as a drunkard or a gangs of youths, he would draw back to my side and take my hand. This made me feel strong. The only thing I could give him that he could not get himself was physical strength. With me he felt safe; we fed off each other.

Quan and I became good friends. He made me feel like a father and he began to trust me. I was careful not to cultivate a friendship where he relied on me, as I did not want him to be upset when I eventually left. Occasionally, I tried to express my affection by offering to buy him a gift. As we passed shops, I was careful to watch if anything caught his eye. I would point to things and ask if he wanted them but he did not seem interested; he would look around self-consciously and usher me away. He would share my food and my company but he would take no tangible thing.

In the daytime, he would take me out in his little fishing tub. No bigger than a large washing basket, the tubs were used to ferry things from boats to the shore. Being so large I would nearly tip the thing over, but Quan's skilled hands somehow always managed to keep us on an even keel. Although we could barely talk to each other, our understanding was good. We had developed a kind of Austanese dialogue which, when accompanied by charades, was effective enough.

The night before I was due to leave, I explained to him that I would be going away. I had expected him to be quite upset, but instead he just smiled and asked, 'Where you go to?' He was not in the least distressed. I suppose loss was an emotion he had learned to cope with years ago. but I was still surprised. Leaving was going to affect me more than it would him.

That evening as I went to meet him at the hotel, I bought Quan a small going-away present, a silver chain to replace the string on which he hung the cross his father had given him. We shared dinner, and, as usual, I walked him back to where he slept in the long grass under the brick wall behind the hotel. As usual, he was reluctant for me to come too close to his little 'house' for fear I would attract attention to it. As we neared the fence Quan checked quickly to make sure no one was watching and then we jumped over.

I took out the gift I had bought and offered it to him. Quan stepped sharply backwards, shaking his head. 'No, no,' he said. 'No souvenir please, no souvenir.'

Bewildered and a little disappointed, I ruffled his hair. Okay sport,' I said, and told him I would meet him tomorrow at the hotel before we left.

That night, rather than returning directly to my hotel as I usually had, I took a stroll along the beach. I could not understand why Quan would not accept my gift. Perhaps he was afraid of commitment, or things that reminded him of good times. Perhaps he did not want to allow himself to get close to people. I could not work it out.

It was getting late and, not wanting to be on the streets alone at night, I decided to catch a trishaw home. As I neared Quan's place I told the driver to pull over and wait. I jumped from the trishaw and, leaning over the fence, placed my gift next to the sleeping boy.

The next morning I packed my bags and took them downstairs to the car. I expected Quan to be there as we had arranged, but he was nowhere to be seen. I told the driver to wait a minute and jogged around the fence to where he slept. I reached the brick wall and climbed over it. He was there, sitting half dazed against the wall, with dried blood on the side of his face and a nasty cut above his left eye. My gift, of course, was gone and I, blissfully unaware of the complexities of life, could not believe my own stupidity.

A SUNKEN-FACED, angular old man tapped his ox on the rump with a stick and it lurched forward jerking the wooden cart behind it. Pivoting unevenly on its bent axle, the cart bobbed its way past the relic of an army Jeep, rusting at the roadside. The old man's progress was painfully slow and yet the purpose in his shuffling step was as dogged as the steady sway of the lumbering ox was inexorable. I felt compelled to wait and watch a full twenty minutes until he had passed out of sight, leaving behind the straight-backed women in bamboo hats picking rice in the rectangular fields.

Twenty years ago Cu Chi was one of the most heavily bombed villages in the history of war but today it was peaceful and quiet. I ate lunch beneath the eucalyptus trees, surrounded by local children who posed for photos and then ran off excitedly to their huts. Looking at the bamboo and wooden shacks, the skinny people, the dusty roads, it seemed miraculous that they ever managed to stave off the Americans. I thought back to a museum in Ho Chi Min City which contained pictures of Cu Chi after the war, totally defoliated, its buildings abandoned and demolished. Some years later the hospitals reported an unusually high rate of birth deformities. I saw photos of children with two heads, cleft palates and some with no faces. The place is full of such ghosts, or perhaps they existed only in my head, their secrets locked in the past, buried with those who died for an ideology which is now, in its turn, dying.

Cu Chi is the starting point of more than 250 kilometres of tunnels begun by Ho Chi Minh in 1943 to thwart the French. The tunnels were extended to an underground city large enough to house an army by the time the Americans had arrived. There were meeting rooms which held up to fifty people, movie theatres, sleeping quarters, bomb shelters, kitchens, and even fully-equipped hospitals. It would have taken the better part of four days to walk the length of it.

My guide Minh wore a white canvas hat with the words 'Welcome To Saigon Tourist', written around the rim. He led me through the back of the village to a small clearing.

'Here,' he said, 'within four metres, is the entrance. You may look but you will not find it.'

Without greenery or extensive ground vegetation, I had thought the tunnels would be easy to find. I searched for fifteen minutes. 'There is no tunnel here,' I said, looking up to our guide.

'You're standing on it,' said Minh, dropping down onto one knee and wiping away the leaves with his hand. He took a stick and began to dig. Eventually he uncovered the head of a bolt and, with some effort, lifted it to reveal a trapdoor about a metre square. 'You will now understand why the Americans had so much trouble spotting them from aeroplanes at 4000 feet,' he said.

From 1968 to 1975 the Americans had tried everything to infiltrate the tunnel system. First they attempted to defoliate the area, assuming this would enable them to locate the entrances from above. It was an expensive tactical error; not only were the entrances almost impossible to locate at ground level, but the Vietnamese only came out at night. When the Americans tried using sniffer dogs, the Vietcong laid fake scents that led into minefields. Every initiative of the Americans was thwarted by the resourceful enemy. When they tried dropping computer-controlled heat-seeking devices over suspected tunnel areas, the Vietcong responded by moving the devices to false targets, often causing the Americans to bomb their own troops.

Although it had been widened to accommodate Western tourists, the tunnel mouth was barely wide enough to fit my hips. Slowly I lowered myself into the dark hole. My legs tingled until I felt the ground. Minh followed, pulling the trapdoor closed behind him.

The darkness was such I couldn't tell if my eyes were open or closed. Muffled sounds echoed from different directions, making it impossible to guess their origins. Unable to orientate myself, I dropped to the ground, and began to crawl.

Remarkably, several Americans and Australians did manage to infiltrate the tunnels but it must have taken indescribable nerve because the majority of entries to the system were booby trapped. Minh told me that sometimes soldiers found what they thought was an entry tunnel, only to pass through the trap door onto a pit of sharpened bamboo spikes. The Vietcong also tied snakes so they dangled from the tunnel ceiling ready to strike the unsuspecting intruder. A wrong turn in the system could mean a 'trip wire' spear through the chest. An intruder might lie there, wedged in for hours before he died, his dead body left as a reminder to any who followed of the futility of the exercise. Other tunnels led in huge circles; unable to orientate himself once inside, the intruder simply circled endlessly until he either suffocated or starved to death.

Crawling along inside the tunnel, my hands became my eyes, feeling their way along the floor, my shoulders rubbed the walls, my head and back scraped the roof. The tunnels were unbearably hot and small.

It took a long time to get the hang of crawling so that I no longer bumped into the sides or the roof. I maintained an even, steady pace, until the guide, Minh, called me to stop. Seconds later he lit a match. When my eyes adjusted I realised we were no longer in the tunnel but in a room. I was dripping with sweat, my back was aching and it was a relief to stand. The room was small but long. 'Maybe twenty soldier sleep here,' Minh said, moving up a set of stairs to push open a trapdoor to the outside. The sudden brightness filled the room and I followed Minh out into the fresh air. He laughed at the sight of my face and pointed to where we had begun. It was only about a hundred metres away. We had been averaging about two metres a minute.

'How long did the soldiers actually spend down the tunnels at one time?' I asked.

'Some came out at nights,' said Minh. 'They never saw daylight. Other men remain in tunnel for three, maybe four year,' was his passing reply.

IN DALAT, Nga, my guide, would often come by my hotel in the mornings and take me for a walk.

'It was my home in the early days,' she said. 'But now it is like a prison. I see buildings where I played and studied as a child, the lake where I walked on Sundays with my family. They are all still here, the same but somehow different. Like me. I am here, I am the same person I was but I am trapped, a prisoner in myself and my country.'

Although Nga was philosophical about life in post-war Vietnam, she harboured a real sadness and at times resentment about where it had left her. In her twenties she had won a scholarship to study in Canada. It would have been the break she needed to establish herself in Vietnam by bringing in overseas dollars but, without explanation, the government refused her a visa to travel. Ever since, she had worked in a poorly paid job she didn't really enjoy. But for her there was never any question of emigrating from Vietnam. She wanted instead to change it, but at thirty-four she felt she was running out of steam.

'After I was refused my scholarship,' she said, 'I tried to stop dreaming. I sent my ambition to prison and tried to live each day as it came.'

Near the end of my visit, Nga took me to the Lake of Lovers, where she had walked with her family. As we made our way through the pine trees, shrieks of laughter rose from excited couples rowing on the lake. She walked slowly, her straight black hair fanning along her collar line with the motion of each step. Although she had been my guide and friend since I had arrived in Vietnam, I didn't really know her at all. She had kept a distance between us, perhaps deliberately, perhaps out of modesty, I didn't know.

'Have you ever been in love?' I asked her.

'Perhaps once.' she replied. 'But it is not good to be in love in times such as these. It fills you with too much expectation.'

I tried not to be judgemental. Her present had become a prisoner of her past, unable to break free from the expectations of her childhood and her learning.

Occasionally, however, she told me of the Vietnam I had not seen in my travels; of the place where she grew up; where she had learned Vietnamese history and poetry from her grandmother. She told me of the coconut palms that grew from the breast of all mothers in the fields, where on hot days the workers would climb their long trunks and cut free coconuts to share the milk. 'A mother's love', she said 'is without expectation; it is more a physical than an emotional thing.'

We rested at the bottom of the hill where a tributary stream trickled into the lake. 'Sometimes', she said 'I think I want to be like the water. To take myself out of my body and out of my country. To live without borders.'

Cambodia

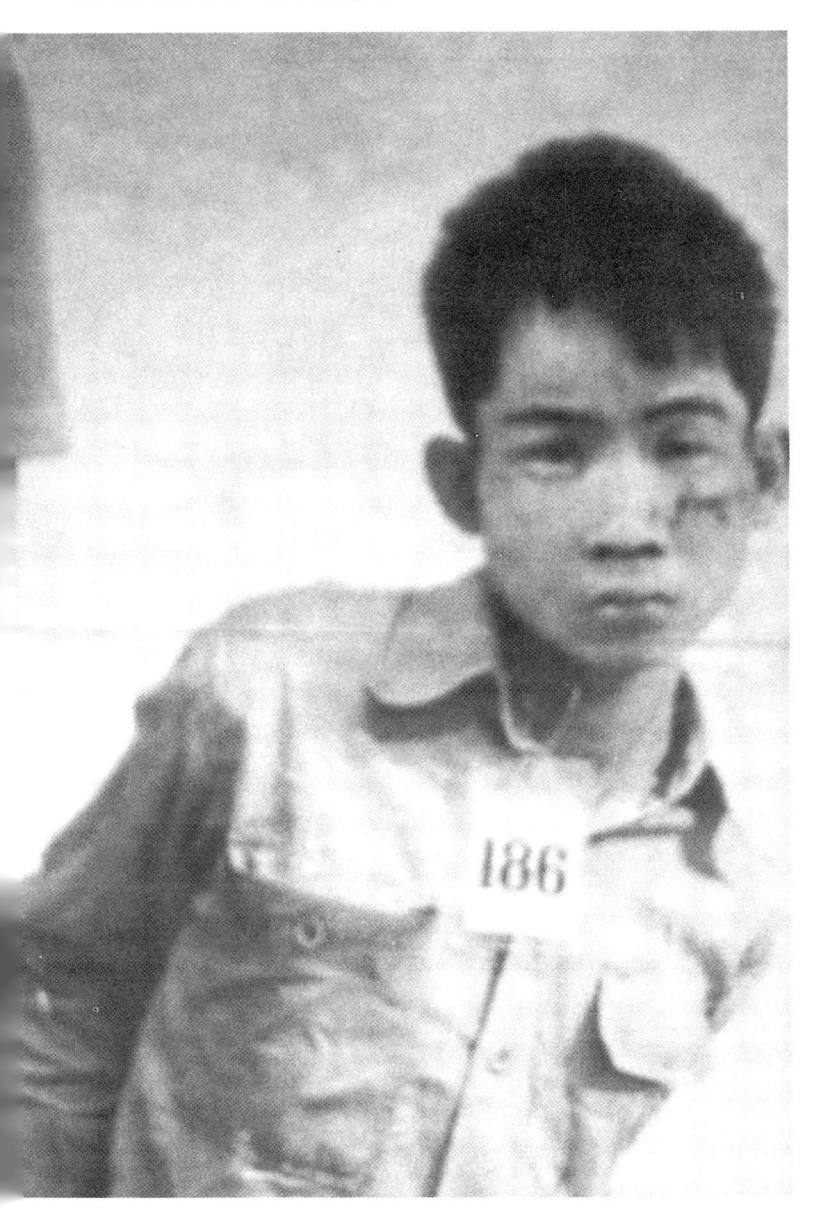

AS WE DROVE through the outskirts of Phnom Penh the gaping doors and vacant windows of gutted houses spoke for themselves. Nga was silent. She had not wanted to come to Cambodia, but I had insisted, as without her, it would have been impossible for me to enter. Ten years ago, while working as a tour guide, she had witnessed the atrocities of the Khmer Rouge and was uncomfortable about returning, even now.

It was perhaps selfish of me to want to go to Cambodia. If I am honest I must admit I was motivated by an obsession with atrocity more than anything else. As a child I was transfixed by the photos of bulldozers pushing bodies into mass graves at Auschwitz. What makes people do such things to other people? I doubted my right to bear witness to what happened in Cambodia but at the same time I felt I must see for myself.

Along the road we were stopped for document checks several times by youths dragging guns as if they were cricket bats. Ten years ago we would have been shot merely for driving the car, but today there was no problem.

I was more fascinated than afraid. I remember one boy, impatient at the car window. He was no more than sixteen. It's a fair bet that he'd had little education, and knew nothing of the rest of the world. Yet he held a gun, and he could have ended my life. Oddly, it was exhilarating. I smiled at him; he smiled back and we drove on.

Phnom Penh is like a big dog that's been kicked too many times. When you get close it seems to shrink away. It's a total atmosphere: a fear that intoxicates everything it touches.

We parked in the centre of town and walked across to the royal palace. Sunshine danced across the Mekong River and darted off at angles from the decorated wall of the Grand Palace, the home of Prince Sihanouk until the US-backed coup of 1970. Here, for generations, Cambodian kings had entertained foreign heads of State and other dignitaries. Parades, festivals and coronations were held in the imposing courtyards under the high-peaked roofs and golden Buddhas. Now, like an old whore, the palace solicits a two dollar entry fee from its clients.

Where Cambodian girls once danced for kings and presidents, grass grows in the cracked paving. A lone man worked at the gate. The stone steps to the coronation hall had been worn down from the passage of millions of feet.

The coronation hall was dark and bare. Single chairs, broken vases and unframed portraits had been awkwardly placed along the walls in a hollow attempt to give the room substance. The throne, ridiculously grand, dominated one end.

In the palace grounds there were two buildings. One, an ornate, open-ended shelter, used to house the royal elephants. The other was a chic reconstruction of a French manor house, where royal guests used to stay. In 1975 the palace grounds were commandeered by the Khmer Rouge for interrogation purposes. Inside each of the buildings there was an overpowering atmosphere, the kind that makes you conscious of your physical being. I sat in chairs, my spine pressing firmly against their backs. I stared at walls, the emptiness pushing on my temples, weighing down my arms: kings had sat here, with all the ceremony that royalty brings: in the same place ordinary citizens, regardless of rank, had been tortured to death.

The balance between beauty and horror was macabre. In their iconoclastic fervour, the Khmer Rouge not only stripped the palace of decor, they had tried to strip the meaning from life. I felt it wherever I moved, heightened occasionally by a piece of lintel or carved wood-work that had escaped the ravage. Outside Nga took my hand and led me onto the stones where kings had walked, the same stones where soldiers had reportedly played football with the severed heads of children.

The main road passing the palace was a wide French boulevard, lined with tall palms and divided by a raised median strip. Running parallel was an esplanade on the banks of the Mekong River. The streets were busy and the people industrious, but there was an air of impermanence. People were unwilling to rebuild and there were no substantial structures. The broken footpaths and gutters had become the houses and workshops for many. It was as if the population was in transit, ready at any time to pack up and disappear.

At night there were no street lights. Cars and motorcycles disappeared at 11 o'clock into a haze of dimly-lit exhaust fumes. The power went off and Phnom Penh folded away into the eerie buzz of generators. From behind closed doors came the lowered voices of families; halos of candle light glowing through closed curtains. The bicycle repairers, fruit sellers, clothes and souvenir stalls were all gone.

We were staying with Nga's friend Meng. She had lived in Phnom Penh for fifty years and was one of the last evacuated in 1975. Her husband, Lon Ni, had been a teacher at the nearby school. She had five children and, by Cambodian standards, a beautiful house. We entered through two iron gates that locked behind us. Wire ran across the top of the fence and the windows were barred.

Nga and I shared a room on the ground floor, looking onto a small courtyard. Through the window, I watched Meng playing with her youngest son. She was a large, broad-footed woman, the type one generally associates with stability. Yet there was a nervousness in her laughter and a hesitancy in her movements.

A calendar hung on the wall read, 'Cambodia; The Land of Smiles, January 1970.' The young girl in the picture, Nga told me, was Meng's first daughter, Mia. She was smiling, holding a bunch of flowers to celebrate the coming of the New Year. Five years later, she and her sister were killed by the Khmer Rouge. Both were beaten to death in front of Meng and her husband. The shock was so great that Meng was unable to speak for three years.

Meng's story is not unique. Nobody went untouched. You see it in the faces. The young look old, smiles are nervous, eyes averted and laughter is frequently accompanied by an uneasy sideways glance. I slept restlessly that night, uncomfortable in the knowledge that Meng's daughter had once slept in this bed.

The following day Nga and Lon Ni took me to see Tuol Sleng, the Pol Pot museum. The building was formerly the school at which Lon Ni had worked. He remembered the day the Khmer Rouge took over.

'Any apprehension my people had about the way we would

be treated was quickly confirmed,' he said. 'They simply walked in with loaded guns and ordered all the children to go home to their parents. We were told there was no further need for this kind of education and that they should not return to school. Teachers who had not fled were rounded up and later killed in their own classrooms.'

Within days the Khmer Rouge had turned the school into a death camp. The lower-floor classrooms became interrogation cells. The top-floor ones were bricked up into prison cells. The assembly hall was transformed into a torture chamber and the playground into an execution ring.

On the wall outside the interrogation rooms hung the original set of ten orders given by Pol Pot to each prisoner. The English translation was crude, but the gist was clear enough :

1. You must answer accordingly to my questions. Don't turn them away.
2. Don't try to hide the facts by making pretexts this and that. You are strictly prohibited to contest me.
3. Don't dare be a fool for you are a chap who dare to thwart the revolution.
4. You must immediately answer my questions without wasting time to reflect.
5. Don't tell me either about your immoralities or the essence of the revolution.
6. While getting lashes or electrification you must not cry out.
7. Do nothing, sit still and wait for my orders. If there is not any order, keep quiet. When I ask you to do something, you must do it right away without protesting.
8. Don't make pretexts about Kampuchea Krom in order to hide the jaw of a traitor.
9. If you don't follow all the above rules, you will get many lashes of the electric wire.
10. If you disobey any point of my regulations you shall get either ten lashes or five shocks of electric discharge.

I read this translation of the rules slowly, wondering how many people had done the same before me and how different the experience might have been if the rules were meant for you.

Photos of the corpses left after the Vietnamese liberation in 1979 hung in the interrogation rooms. Every room had a metal bed with hand and foot racks, open barely wide enough to fit the wrists and ankles of a child. Dried blood, and acid from the car batteries used during electric-shock treatment still stained the floor.

Along from the interrogation room, in what was formerly the library, were more photos of some of Pol Pot's victims. No larger than swap cards, they filled all four walls. I stood in the middle of the room and turned, watching them blur into an anonymous collage, but each time I stopped and focused, the staggering atrocity hit. Each face had a name, a family, a history. Men, women, children: the suffering was unspeakable.

The outline of the figure eight, the original number of the room in its school days, was still just visible on the door. It is now known as the room of skulls. There were piles of clothing belonging to the dead; in another corner, the photo of a mass grave; the skulls, like the discarded houses of Phnom Penh, stand in rows. On the far wall hang the remains of an old chalk board; the statistics on it no longer educate children, but document their deaths.

The rectangular stone building was originally designed to look out over the playground, so in the facing cells the prisoners had no option but to watch their fellow captives tortured and eventually killed.

'Psychologically, they were dead long before they were ever killed,' Lon Ni said.

The ropes used by the Khmer Rouge for hangings dangled in threes from a large metal frame. Under each noose was a huge terra-cotta pot filled with water. Victims were tied with their hands behind their backs, hoisted up so their arms dislocated at the shoulders and then lowered into the water until they drowned.

Lon Ni has returned to his school only twice since the liberation. For him it represented the decline of his country more poignantly than anything else.

'Half a generation have either been wiped out or educated in the ways of violence,' he said. 'They are still alive but they live without hearts.'

As we left the school, we were silent. A few children played in the courtyard. Some sat quietly on graves. Others laughed excitedly on a swing from a bar where people used to be hanged. I watched as they were chased away by the museum guard. They ran, laughing, bringing to mind the image of Meng's daughter and rekindling faded echoes of happier times in the empty playground.

I will never forget Cambodia. One impression in particular will never leave me: an image of a beaten man close to death, his expression blank, beyond fear. He had lost his soul. That such a face could exist on this Earth makes a mockery of beauty and a liar of understanding. Yet history will tell us it is the perpetual state of humankind to coexist in misery and happiness. You try to understand, struggle with philosophies and ideas of right and wrong, and good and bad, and just when you think you are getting close it is all blown away in an emotionally overwhelming instant where philosophies don't exist.

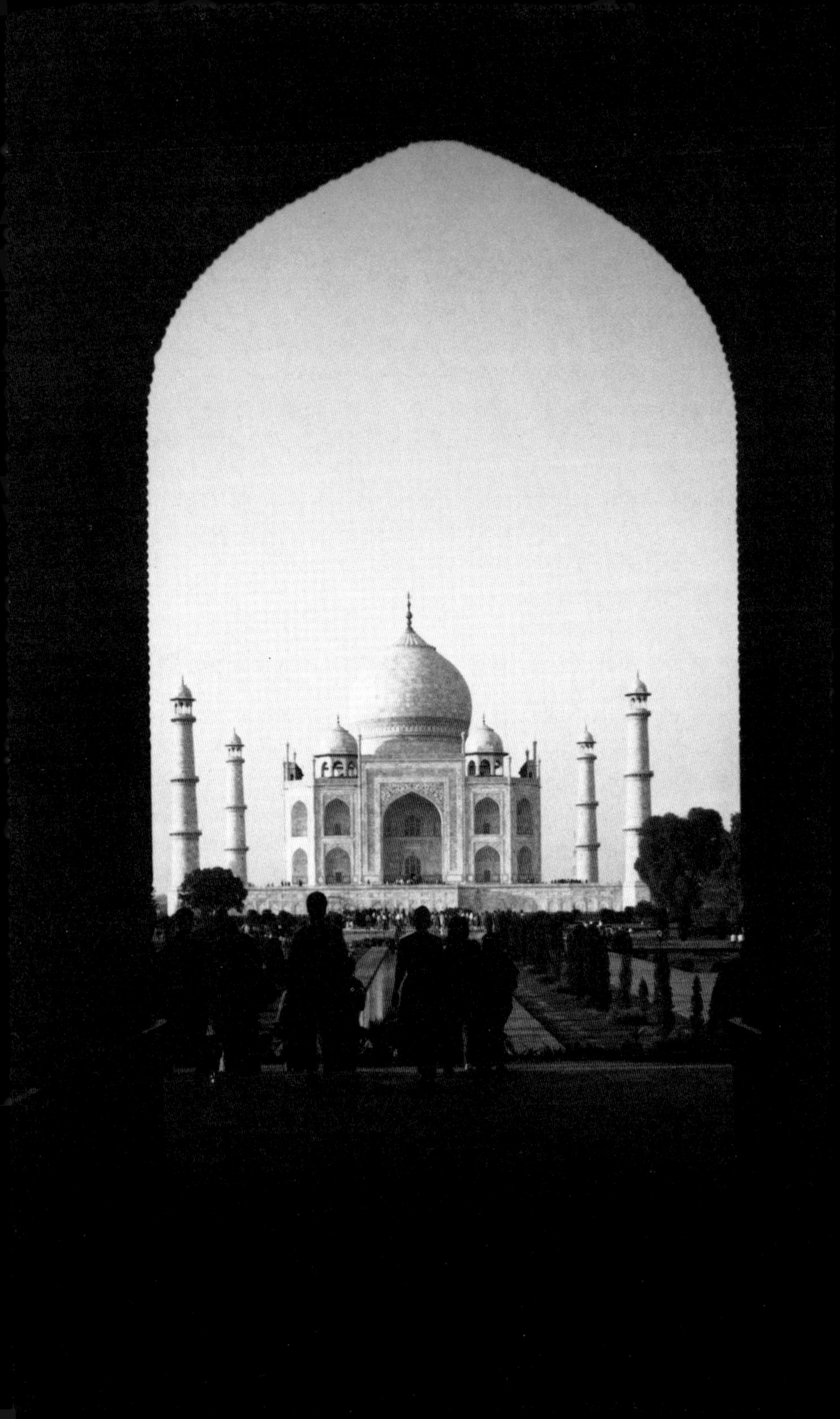

India

THE BUS WAS LATE and it was swelteringly hot as I waited at the front of New Delhi's Indira Gandhi Airport with a small Indian man. The other backpackers had climbed on a bus that had left twenty minutes before. The Indian had assured me that it was not my bus and stupidly, I had bowed to local knowledge and let it go. I was already beginning to regret my high ideals of travelling through India without a guide book.

'When does my bus come?' I asked the man indignantly. He looked up, a little bewildered.

'It has already gone,' he said, rolling his head from side to side.

'But you told me that was not my bus,' I protested.

'It is far too hot for a bus,' said the man, ignoring my protest. 'Come, it just so happens I have my taxi here. I will drive you to Connaught Place myself,' he said, as though he were doing me some great favour. I was too hot to argue and got into the taxi.

In Delhi I got a bed on the roof of a hostel. The place was full of backpackers returning from or heading out on expeditions. With amazing recall, they reeled off complicated names and provinces and places they said I must visit. No one mentioned Sikkim. It is in the north east of India, between the kingdoms of Bhutan and Nepal, at the foot of the Himalayas. I wanted at some stage to visit Bhutan, and Sikkim seemed as good a place to begin as any.

Leaving Delhi was easier said than done. After several false starts I decided to assign myself one task a day. The Indians are notorious for paperwork and red tape and the only way to keep your sanity is to give in to it. I stood in queues for hours only to reach the end and find it was the wrong queue; I watched people push in and out of lines ahead of me without protest.

I had to make a written application for a visa into Sikkim. When I submitted it, I was told it must be written out again, this time in red. I was told three different arrival and departure times for the same train. I had to stand in a queue to buy a ticket to join the queue for tickets, but no one could tell me where to catch the train. Finally I was told I needed a recommendation from the 'Australian Embassy' (High Commission) to get a stamp on my visa for Sikkim. I hailed a taxi and negotiated a price for the trip. It was too much but I was past caring.

When we arrived I got out and paid the driver. 'Enjoy you skiing,' he said. I was puzzled. The man drove off. I turned to go to the gates and nearly died with frustration at the sight of the huge sign on them, reading, 'Welcome to the Austrian Embassy; Citizens Only'.

In the evenings I sat on the roof of my guesthouse, listening to other travellers' tales of woe in India. I had been there a week when it struck me that no one else in the hostel was really doing anything. Many of them had been there for three months and didn't look like leaving. During the days they sat downstairs drinking warm Coke and smoking drugs. At night they came upstairs and either talked of their travels or bitched about Delhi.

On my last evening the proprietors of the hostel removed the canvas tarpaulin that had been our roof. About twelve of us slept on the roof in beds that had been crammed together to accommodate us all. That night the rains came. It rained harder than I have ever seen for about fifteen minutes and then, suddenly, it stopped. None of us moved. Everyone and everything was drenched. I looked across at the bloke next to me. He looked bemused, stringy beads of wet hair hanging across his forehead. He had been here for six months.

'India, only in bloody India,' he said, glancing up to where the tarpaulin used to hang, then laying his head back on his drenched pillow.

THE OVERNIGHT TRAIN from Delhi to Siliguri was crowded, even by Indian standards. Despite having booked a sleeper well in advance, I arrived at the compartment to find my seat already occupied by not one but two other men. I asked them to move and, typically, they ignored me. I showed them my ticket. They looked at each other, shrugged and produced identical tickets. I sat on the floor.

We shared the cabin with a family. In all there were eleven people and only six seats. As well there was the luggage: crates, boxes, suitcases, pets and bicycles. The Indians brought the lot. They stuffed it under seats, in overhead racks, on the floor, in the passageways and on their knees. The train was a microcosm of parts of the country: smelly, dirty, overcrowded and going nowhere in a hurry.

We arrived in Siliguri to discover that the trains had gone on strike. No one could tell me what the problem was, or when the trains would run again. Lack of motion when travelling is frustrating. But I could not leave the platform for fear of the train arriving. I set up camp and began to read E. M. Forster's *A Passage To India*.

The train to take me from Siliguri to Darjeeling, where I was to catch the connecting bus for Sikkim, took two days to arrive. In the interim, I sat and watched as people filled the platform, the station house and the street outside. Perhaps this was why Indians took everything on a train with them. Beside me, a family had just lit a fire and was beginning to boil water for breakfast. They had knives, forks, pots and pans laid out all around their sleeping mats. On the other side, a mother was washing her children in a metal bath. I ate an egg and drank chlorine-flavoured water.

When the train finally pulled in, it was bedlam on the platform. I had never thought myself capable of pushing over a woman or a child, but there was no other way to get on board. Inside, it was impossibly crowded. People sat six to a double seat. Others stood, clinging to each other on top of luggage on the floor. The carriage stank of urine. I made my way to the back of the train, stepping on people, animals and anything else I could put my feet on, and locked myself in the toilet. It stank even more than the carriage.

The train travelled the entire seventy-four kilometres up the mountains at walking pace. From my perch on the toilet, I watched as we passed through the highland villages. As the train entered a town, local children would come running out of houses and side streets. Suddenly two hands would appear on the window ledge, followed by a smiling face. They would ride for a few kilometres, hanging on the outside of the train, then drop off at the next village.

Sometimes the train stopped at a station and just when it seemed impossible that they could fit in any more people, a new sea of dotted foreheads and old suitcases would somehow squeeze into the carriages. I was never to see an Indian turn away from a train because it was too crowded.

I stuck my head out of the window. Smoke and ash filled my face. With each curve those hanging on the side of the train leaned back on outstretched arms. At bridges, legs, arms and torsos sailed past the window and luggage was tossed from the roof as people sitting on the roof hurriedly disembarked to avoid decapitation.

The higher we went the colder it became. The village dress changed and people now wore hats and gloves. The Himalayas began to appear through the window, my first sighting of them. Huge ravines folded away into each other, silver rivers ran like raindrops down a window pane, weaving their way between the valleys that lay beneath the straggly wigs of the snow-capped peaks. For the first time, I saw that India was beautiful.

The door to the toilet was forced open. A man appeared and began to load his luggage inside. Without even acknowledging me he came in and locked the door behind him. I nodded to him and moved across from the toilet to the window. He lifted his sarong and began to urinate, missing the toilet as often as he hit it. When he had finished he lay down on top of his bags. I leaned forward and stared out the window at the mountains, while the streams of his urine sloshed in long lines over the floor and onto my feet.

The man fell asleep, impervious to the smell and cramped conditions. He was middle-aged and unshaven. His skin was dirty, his nails thick and yellow. He was dressed in a white wrap and wore rubber shoes. I wondered how he could sleep while passing such scenery, but to him, I guessed, the Himalayas weren't spectacular; they were home and, to him, the train was not crowded, it was normal.

And so it is with India. To the Westerner, what seems an endlessly disorganised, hopeless and yet beautiful country is, to the Indian, home. The hordes of ringed fingers that clutch at anything stable in the carriage in front, the feet that stand on anything, the eternal smiles and the endless chatter that carries on into the night are as Indian as the Himalayas and, for me, as inaccessible.

These beautiful old steam trains run, not because they are beautiful nor because they're old, but simply because they run. Traditional dress is not worn because it's traditional but because it does not need to change. In India things happen because they do, not because they should.

THE RICE PADDIES cut into the hillside rose like giant steps into the clouds. As the fog became heavier visibility decreased, the bus changed down to second, then first. It laboured until, slowly, sunlight began to dance with the mist and we were above the clouds at 11 000 feet.

All thoughts of my train journey and the frustrations of the past fortnight disappeared. To the east, the snow-capped peaks of the world's third highest mountain, Kanchenjunga, towered a further 5000 metres above us. To the west the Chumbri Valley, which borders Nepal, Tibet and Bhutan, wound itself along the ridges of the Himalayan Ranges. It was the India for which I had searched: a spiritual place.

I spent two days in Gangtok, the capital of Sikkim, where I got information about visiting the local monastery at Rumtek. I was excited about the visit and yet conscious that my travels were losing direction. I was finding it difficult to be with myself. At first I had thought it would be liberating, to be guided solely by my own judgments but, it had proven a burden. All my life, I had been performing for others, seeking praise, looking for self-assurance through positive reinforcement by others. Now, alone in unfamiliar territory, I was lost. I needed somebody to tell me I was doing okay; that what I was doing was worthwhile. Instead, each morning I woke up alone, without any rules.

The bus to Rumtek took an hour. It was a comforting ride. The hustle and bustle of India was behind me. Here, high above a quickly changing world of poverty, war and corruption, Tibetan and Indian monks had been seeking enlightenment for centuries. I felt there was a kind of cultural inertia in their ancient rituals and static society, which was the result of a religious contentment as stable as the mountains in which it was set.

In the monastery courtyard the hollow 'om' sounds of young monks chanting their mantras echoed so solemnly they almost had a physical presence.

Omge Tashy strolled slowly across the yard, his hands tucked inside his sleeves. All around him young shaven-headed boys bobbed rhythmically against the walls. Omge was thirty years old and had been at Rumtek for twenty-one years. I had met him the day before, in Gangtok, and he had invited me to spend some time at the monastery. It was evening when I arrived.

That night, in a room overlooking the valley and the lights of Gangtok below, I lay in bed and thought of my progress. A candle flickered on the ledge, a freezing breeze blew in through the open window. I was invigorated. I was alive. I was sleeping in a monastery alone in the foothills of the Himalayas but, more than anything, I was me. Try as I might on this journey, I could not get away from it: my past was dictating my being so much I could not touch the present. Smells, sights and sounds conjured in me images and events in Australia; I tried many times to let them go but I could not. I did not know how to, or perhaps I was scared.

I wrapped myself in a blanket and sat across the window ledge with the wind blowing in my face. Beneath the blanket I was warm. It is like travel: you wrap your morality, your most precious philosophies in a blanket and take them into the world. The winds of other countries and cultures blow on your face but inside you stay warm, believing your truth to be universal. Your blanket is tolerance; keep it wrapped tightly and your truths will remain for ever; allow it to unfold, expose your truths to the winds and watch them blow away one by one until that which remains is all you have.

At five the following morning Omge came to wake me. He had asked me to join his students, who were preparing for meditation. It was bitterly cold as I followed Omge, dressed only in orange robes and slip-on sandals, into the monastery courtyard. There were no sounds except the shuffling of our feet. Behind him, the rising sun speared his elongated shadow to the ground. The fluffy grey clouds on which the monastery seemed to float began to rise slowly from the valley.

Inside, Omge knelt before a huge glass cabinet. I sat at the back and watched. The cabinet was divided into one thousand compartments, each containing a golden image of Buddha. There was incense in the air, Omge lit a candle, its flame reflected one thousand times, creating a glowing halo, beneath which he knelt motionless for over an hour.

Above his head, long cotton scrolls hung from high beams. A prayer wheel stood motionless in the corner and cushions lay scattered on the floor. It was dark. I could never be happy here, I thought, which was perhaps the message Omge was trying to give me. In the Western world we spend a disproportionately large amount of time catering to secondary comforts. We ignore a truth we face in the mirror every day: before anything else we live inside ourselves. From my limited understanding, this is the Buddhist message: learn to carpet your soul before you carpet your house; understand the difference between happiness and contentment.

When he had finished he snuffed out the candle and rose to leave, not looking at me as he passed. I got up and followed him.

I was full of questions. 'Omge,' I began.

Omge turned and raised his finger to his lips.

At 7.30 the monks had breakfast together in a large hall. The symphony of clicking spoons and scuffing feet sounded rather like a Scout camp. A head monk ladled stingy serves of porridge from a great pot. Younger monks pushed in front of each other, and perhaps the only discernible difference between them and other boys their age was that they were not wearing shoes, despite the freezing cold floor.

After breakfast the boys went off to their studies and I returned to the monastery with Omge.

'I cannot know what you are looking for,' Omge said. 'Such a thing is impossible. I can tell you only that you will not find it here. You are like many who visit Rumtek looking for answers. You will leave disillusioned. We do not have any answers here. I can only show you where to look and how to look, but of course you do not have the time.'

Omge was right. I had come here hoping that things would suddenly become clear; hoping I would find direction and understand the purpose of my travels, but I found myself so wrapped in the Western preoccupation with instant success and finite answers that I had become blind to the Buddhist idea that understanding is a continuous and constantly deepening process. Buddhists do not travel in one direction towards a goal, the layers of their lives go up and down, backwards and forwards. My life, however, has always been spent in pursuit of a goal, heading in one direction, so when confronted with an ideal diametrically opposed to my own, I am forced to destroy it, rather than let it change my course and alter my goal.

Omge's room was cosy compared with the others. He had posters on the walls, a thick rug on the floor and photos of himself in different countries on his desk. One wall had a shelf full of books and cassettes were lined up next to a ghetto-blaster.

'Whatever happened to non-attachment?' I said, picking up a Rolling Stones tape and sliding it into the deck.

'None of this I need,' Omge said. 'If it were gone tomorrow I would be no poorer than today.'

'So if a burglar came in here tonight and you caught him stealing your tape deck, you wouldn't stop him?'

'No,' Omge said. 'I would give him the tapes as well. A cassette player is no good without tapes.'

His flippant answer annoyed me deeply.

'So if I took your tape deck now, you wouldn't stop me?'

'On the contrary,' Omge said. 'I would give it to you so you could go in peace.'

Bullshit, I thought to myself and walked over to the tape deck and took it off the shelf.

'Please,' Omge said, unplugging the cord and handing it to me. 'Take this too. It is no good without it. I have no batteries.'

I was inexplicably angry: furious with the simplicity of Omge's reactions; and yet I could not leave. The tape deck was heavy. I thought of myself lugging it onto trains, buses and up highways for the next few years. The idea was ridiculous.

'I don't need it,' I said to Omge.

'Me neither,' he shrugged.

AT HOWRAH STATION, a buffalo lay jackknifed in the car park. Still trapped between the cart poles, its chest rose and fell in sharp movements and its moist nostrils glistened and flared. Its eyelids flickered and after a final attempt to lift its head, the great beast died. Just as I stopped to look, the hordes of people leaving the station behind me surged forward, pushing their way into the street. Like a non-swimmer struggling in the surf, I floundered, as wave after wave of people lifted my feet and carried me in their direction.

'This is Calcutta,' said a passing man who had noticed my distress. 'You can't stop here.'

The Hooghley Bridge is the major access into Calcutta. At any time, day or night, it is jam-packed with activity: cars spewing exhaust, trams and buffalo carts, pedestrians and lopsided buses with passengers clinging like bees to their doors and windows. I was just one of half a million who would cross it that day to join twelve million on the other side. It's like putting the population of Australia into metropolitan Melbourne. You can't help thinking that something, somewhere soon has to give.

Everything is taken to extremes. Tyres bulge, axles bow, wheels are splayed, as every conceivable mode of transport is loaded beyond its capacity with people or produce. The footpaths rise in lumps and cracks, as if people were trying to push their way out from underneath. Doors barely hang on their hinges. Cars are not out of petrol until they stop. A green light means go, until it's red; there is no such thing as orange. At meal times the rims of bowls are licked and the bottoms of cups drained. Everyone and everything is moving. On every face, on every corner, is the look of people straining to keep up.

There are those, however, such as the female porters, scurrying back and forth across the bridge, who seem to have come to terms with their city. Faces half hidden by saris, the purpose and resilience of their bodies gives the impression that perhaps life is bearable after all. In their slip-on rubber shoes, they swagger back and forth across this long, crowded bridge up to twenty times a day. They are among the few who appear to take pride in their work. Calcutta is their city and, like the mothers of naughty children, they resent it for all its flaws and the suffering it causes, but love it nonetheless.

In the city centre, Calcutta's former elegance is barely holding on. There are still remnants of the Raj as there are in much of India but they are run down and poorly maintained. The once beautiful Edwardian and Victorian buildings now stand in slatternly squalor on the street corners, and, rather than conjuring up images of former glories, they serve only to emphasise the dilapidation and decay.

I spent the day grasping for some redeeming feature, some magical little piece of India which Calcutta had hidden away for its visitors; but I found nothing. The majesty of the Taj, the philosophy of Gandhi, the mysticism of religion, the spiritualism of the Ganges, did not exist here for me. Calcutta's soul was being peddled on the pretext that somehow its past could help it abstain from the realities of its future.

In side streets, children defecate where they sleep, sewerage drains overflow, animals die and are left to rot. Old women sift through garbage piles. They do not pick as one might when searching for an item lost in a rubbish bin. They delve deeply, on hands and knees, looking for anything which might be of value.

Initially I could not help staring. I tried hard not to judge what I saw, not to apply my morality in a place where it had no frame of reference, but I could not stop thinking that I would never allow myself to sink so low. At the time, I knew the thought was naive, but the reality was inescapable.

After only a few days in Calcutta I noticed a change in my attitude. The rubbish-picking beggars were everywhere: a fact of life. The more often I walked past them the more hard-hearted I became. Rationalisation became easier.

'My little bit won't help.'

'I will only encourage them by giving.'

'He doesn't really need it.'

'It's not my problem anyway.'

'I've got enough worries looking after myself, let alone somebody else.'

Some travellers I met even took pride in not giving, as if they were somehow doing the beggars a favour. 'A little lesson in capitalism and self-sufficiency.' In reality they were doing themselves the favour. To give is to acknowledge there is something to give to, and, this being the case, the traveller assumes an uncomfortable burden of his or her own.

Outside Mother Theresa's Home for the Destitute and Dying, I observed two ends of a scale. On one side, the old wearily lined up for their daily wash and hand-out. On the other, children tugged at my shirt tails; their little hands sifted through my pockets. 'One rupee, one rupee,' they called. They were bold. Some had no shame, a fact which often won them their spoils. They earned their living through their ability to evoke sympathy; self-mutilation and an unsanitary way of life were designed to meet this end. It was depressing. The only hope these children have for survival is to swim deeper into the sewer that is Calcutta. Any attempt to rise above it would exclude them from their one means of surviving in it.

Over a period of days from my balcony, I watched a thousand little cameos of Calcutta, each as hopeless as the previous one. I began to ask the simplistic questions Westerners tend to ask. Why are these people so poor? Why is there no food and shelter? Why don't they keep themselves and the streets clean? Why are they so unhygienic? Why don't they care about the environment? I began to apply my own standards; I detested their apathy. Even worse, I detested the people themselves.

The answers to my questions came slowly. The longer I stayed in Calcutta, the more I felt at home. At first I began to litter. Putting rubbish in bins seemed pointless. What few there were, were overflowing, and the garbage would only end up in the river or back on the streets. Next I began to eat without washing my hands. The plates and even the food itself were dirty. It seemed a futile exercise. I began to drink local water if I couldn't buy bottled. Often I couldn't wash because the water was turned off.

Inevitably, I got sick.

Amoebic dysentery. The first bout lasted around six days. I was living in a private room in a backpackers' hostel when it hit.

My stomach and head ached so badly my bones hurt. I spent the whole first day throwing up. I couldn't even keep down my own saliva. On the second day I lost control of my bowels. I was running a fever and felt too weak to move. I put a towel underneath me and lay for hours in my own excrement.

On the third day the landlord came up to see why I had not paid my rent. I still had a fever but I had managed to clean myself earlier that morning. The landlord brought me some water and said if I was not better in two days I should go to hospital.

Each day seemed hotter than the last. Each night I lay drenched in sweat, unable to move, as though someone had passed skewers through my bones. The stench of the city drains wafted through the window. Mosquitos buzzed in my ears, and bit me undisturbed. The noise outside was constant and piercing. The seconds crawled by, each one a burden. When sleep finally came, it was total: both body and mind had surrendered. I don't know how long I was out but I have no recollection at all of the next two days.

When I woke, I felt much better although I was desperately thirsty. I took a drink from the manager's water bottle and shuffled gingerly to the bathroom to wash my face. On the way out I glanced at the mirror; the face that peered back gaunt and listless was not my own. I spent another day in bed, so relieved to be out of pain. For the six days I had thought of nothing but my pain and the universe existed nowhere but within me; social etiquette and personal hygiene meant nothing. I had been reduced to the basic instinct for self-preservation and inadvertently been offered a glimpse of what it was like to delve into a garbage pile on all fours.

When I left Calcutta, I took with me a whole new perspective. During my week of sickness, Calcutta had not even blinked. It had never stopped. Thousands had died. Thousands more had been born. Millions had been sick and suffered worse than I had and millions more would do so. Calcutta is a runaway train and the faster it goes the harder it is to stop.

Nepal

THE OVERLAND TRIP from Calcutta to Kathmandu took three days and would have been beautiful except that for most of them I was being sick out of the bus window. Each bump was excruciating and several times I lost control of my bowels and was forced to get off the bus in deference to the noses of my fellow passengers. On the final occasion, just 80 kilometres out of Kathmandu, the bus took off before I'd had time to claim my luggage. I watched helplessly, my pants full of shit as all I owned in the world disappeared up the road on top of the lop-sided bus. After I had cleaned myself I boarded the next bus which, as luck would have it, arrived at the terminus just as my previous bus was unloading. I managed to beat the local porters to it as it was thrown off the bus and, slinging it gratefully over my shoulder, I headed into town. .

Kathmandu was a contradiction. The Nepalese were striving to break into the '90s while the Westerners were yearning for the '60s. Musk and incense mingled with fast-food smells of hot doughnuts and hamburgers. Street hawkers grabbed my sleeves. 'Hash, dope, change money,' they whispered while pulling me into alleyways alongside the watchful eyes of Rambo and the Dalai Lama who vied for poster space in shop windows.

Though I had come to Nepal to trek, I was still very weak and unsure I could make it any distance. I was resigning myself to a week's recovery in Kathmandu when I noticed a sign in a shop window advertising horse treks.

At first the owner seemed reluctant to hire me a horse, but when I told him I was from Australia, his eyes lit up. 'Snowy River Man!' he exclaimed.

'Well, why not.' I replied.

'You leave from Phokara on Wednesday,' he said signing my trekking visa and pushing it back over the counter to me.

It was silent as I headed out along the shore of Lake Phewa, my small white pony swaggering from side to side, steam rising from its nostrils. The water was still and all around the valley rose the huge peaks of the Annapurnas. Nature seemed powerful and I felt as though I were intruding. The lake path soon turned up the mountain side, leaving the village to gradually disappear below. My horse slipped occasionally on the stone path, sending little rocks clattering down the hillside. My head was spinning, with a combination of sickness and exhilaration.

It took two hours to reach the little village of Sarankot at the top. From here the Annapurna Mountains come into full view. I tied my horse and walked to the cliff edge, where I sat for hours, small and insignificant, watching the clouds roll across the peaks while the cold stiff winds blew into my face. I felt vulnerable and alone and yet I could feel my strength returning.

For the next two days I rode in a circle through the little Nepalese villages, stopping occasionally to eat or sleep. The villagers are used to trekkers. Their little smoke-filled, wooden huts always had a pot of something cooking. In the yards pigs and chickens ran free and children played draughts with bottle tops. At night it was bitterly cold but sometimes I would take my sleeping bag outside.

There is something curative in simple living. For four days I did not have to think. I followed the track, I slept when I was tired and I ate when I was hungry. Out here I was anonymous and insignificant. I think I began to understand why people want to climb mountains; to rise out of the world. At the foot of one of these 8000 metre peaks you are nothing – on top you are the highest self-propelled person on earth, in many ways you are climbing out of humanity, out of yourself, until it is just you alone with nature.

I spent the final night back at Sarankot and left early in the morning. About halfway down the mountain it began to rain. I watched the storm blow in along the valley, falling, first in large penetrating drops, and then in sheets like a blanket across the lake. I did not want to hide from it. I let it fill my body, massaging my head and chest, cleansing me of my sickness. At the bottom, as my horse and I crossed onto the lake track, lightning flashed over mountain tops, thunder cracked up the valley, and the horse bolted. I closed my eyes, fell into its rhythm and, with the rain beating into my face, I let it run.

WHEN I RETURNED, Kathmandu was on the boil. Since I had been away, the normally peaceful capital had erupted in protests and violence against the king. I decided to take a taxi into town and see what had happened. The taxi passed through several road-blocks, stopping only to acknowledge the guards who peered in through the windows then waved us on. The outskirts of town were a jumble of overturned vehicles. There was smashed glass everywhere. Angry people streamed earnestly and steadily down the road. Eyes peered from every window. Shopkeepers had closed their shutters and gesticulating old men stood reviewing the events in doorways. Large, green, army trucks filled with the helmeted heads of the riot police were stationed on every street corner. Pedestrians glanced up apprehensively as they passed. Others stood, watching curiously like birds, ready at any minute to pick, or at the first sign of trouble, to fly.

The nearer we came to the town the more the footpath crowd spilled onto the roads. They were coming from everywhere, their emotional intensity rising visibly. The distinction between road and footpath disappeared; people formed into groups. Their pace quickened. The crowd around us assumed direction, growing in confidence as it grew in size. Soon my vision was obscured by the throng and the car was rocked sideways as often as it moved forward. Shopkeepers and farmers who, a week ago had smiled and welcomed me into their homes as individuals, now marched as a group. I sensed that at any moment they might snap and overturn the car.

'It's coming pretty fast,' said the driver, as he turned towards me.

'What is?' I asked. 'What's been going on?'

'Democracy,' he said proudly.

The 'Quest for Democracy', as they called it, had been causing unrest for months. When I had arrived, King Barendrah had twice ordered a curfew to keep demonstrating students off the streets, but they had persisted. Before I had left for Pokhara I had heard rumours that ringleaders had been taken to prison and killed.

KANCHANJUNGA
TRAVELLERS
SERVICE
HAIR
Center
Dresser
THAHITY SHOE SHOP

The taxi had come to a virtual standstill and the driver turned to me a little nervously.

'Democracy no place for a taxi,' he laughed, and in typical Asian style he pressed his hand flat on the horn and turned the taxi off the main road and into a cul-de-sac.

From where we had parked, it was impossible to judge the size of the crowd, or, due to the random design of the streets, in which direction it was heading. But clearly it was angry and its energy was contagious.

'We want Demo-cracy. We want Demo-cracy,' they chanted in a fist-thrusting euphoric mantra that echoed up the road.

We got out of the taxi. 'They plenty serious this time,' said the driver, hastily locking the doors. 'Plenty biggest crowd.' He seemed to gain strength from the unity of the crowd as if it proved the legitimacy of the cause.

'I leave you here now, Boss,' he said excitedly. 'No charge for taxi. This a great day for Nepal, come!' He ripped his T-shirt off and ran down the road towards the crowd, disappearing into the anonymous kaleidoscope of pummelling torsos.

I was not so excited. None of the seven so-called communist parties, which had established themselves as alternatives to the monarchs who had ruled the Nepalese for generations, seemed to have any policy other than that of a party freely elected for the people. Hardly a communist ideal, their political naivety seemed a tenuous masthead for a movement which had gathered such support. Caught up in the momentum of the protest, it appeared that the Nepalese had created something they could not stop. Ideology and logic took a back seat to the feelings of immense power in a people all too aware of what they were running from, but with no idea where they were heading.

For the next hour I allowed myself to be swept along through the streets of Kathmandu. Some sprinkled water from the windows, to cool people down. Shopkeepers handed out drinks in doorways, losing their cups each time. The streets vibrated, the crowd bounced in unison. On every face was excitement, in every clenched fist anger, all packed in by the buildings that channelled us to the royal palace.

Protected by those around them, people discarded their inhibitions; they sensed power, moving together as individuals but releasing energy as a group. They fed off each other. Even Westerners on holiday, who had no idea what it was all about, became involved, chanting as though they had worked in the fields of Nepal and been exploited by the king for years.

It was not my war. There was something unsettling about being caught up in such an unstoppable motion. I hated not being free to move – it was much the same, I imagine, as being trapped in a football-crowd crush. Hands pinned by my sides, my legs often lifted from the ground, I was caught in a beast I couldn't control. Slowly I edged my way along the side of the road where the police had set up barricades. I managed to get a leg up and swing myself on to an overhanging balcony, from which I could see the whole street.

Red-and-white Nepalese flags fluttered under the sagging overhead wires which crisscrossed the streets. Further down, the road fanned out into a roundabout. The more open streets that surrounded the palace had been blocked off by the Army and guards stood ready to divert protesters as they marched around the block again. The pressure was building.

Then suddenly it happened. A protester fell, was pushed, charged; who knows? Like a burst water pipe, the barricade was broken. The soldiers panicked. Chants turned to screams and the sharp crack of rifle fire filled the air. The crowd broke up and people tried to run, peeling off the main road in whatever direction they could, breaking through the flashing sticks of police lines and scampering down side streets, up walls and along alleys as best they could. Unity gave way to chaos. People punched and kicked, clambering over each other as their instant priority became shelter. Men threw women out of doorways and attempted to kick the doors down.

Tear gas quickly followed. People thrashed wildly, like fish out of water, bumping into each other as they ran with jackets pulled over heads to avoid the smoke.

My eyes and throat began to burn. I had to move. I jumped blindly down from the balcony into the fast-emptying street. With my shirt tied around my face, I ran with the crowd around the corner. The last thing I saw was the green jacket of a policeman and his bamboo pole as it cracked down on the side of my head.

THE HOSPITAL FOYER WAS CHAOS. A teenager lay, stripped from the waist down, in front of me. Blood ran in two trickles from a hole in his thigh. His shirt was stained red, his cut-off jeans discarded on the floor beside him. A pale arm hung over the edge of his bed, his eyes were rolled back in their sockets.

I stared, unable to break my gaze. My head was throbbing. All around me people were rushing and yelling. Along the walls, rows of makeshift drips hung between mattresses on the floor. Ambulance men rushed in with stretchers, their heels clipping on the floor as they went.

'Excuse me, sir,' said a voice behind me. 'But are you English?' I sat up. A sharp-faced young man laid his hand on my shoulder.

'No,' I replied, 'I'm Australian.' It hurt to speak. My jaw felt disconnected from my skull.

'You were knocked unconscious just a couple of blocks from here,' he said. 'You'll be okay. It's your friend I'm worried about.'

'My friend?' I said, puzzled.

'Yes, the other English chap. He's in a bad way. We simply have to get him to the other hospital or I'm afraid he will not make it.'

'Well,' I said, a little confused, 'I'm willing to help, but I'm travelling alone. I've no idea who this fellow is.'

'His name's Reid,' said the doctor. 'Andrew Reid. They carried him in here next to you. I presumed you were friends.'

I was still staring at the boy opposite. They had placed a sheet over most of his body and only the feet protruded. He'd lost a shoe. I visualised him tying his laces before he left home that morning and wondered if he had done so willing to die for the cause he was going to support.

'Mr Reid. Sir. Will you help?'

'Yes, yes, of course. What's the problem?'

'He's been shot through the leg. I don't think we can save it. We'll have to operate here, but if he makes it, well,' — he glanced around — 'our facilities are already stretched to the limit. I don't know how long we'll be able to keep him.'

Two days ago I had not a care in the world, and now a doctor was telling me someone's life depended upon me. On the doctor's advice I rang the British Embassy to see if they could organise an ambulance for tomorrow morning. They said they would do all they could but if a curfew was in place, which seemed likely, they would not be able to do anything. We would just have to wait until he was out of surgery.

The hospital was filled to overflowing, and the doors had been locked. It was full and then some. Everywhere I looked, even in the foyer, were wounded people needing attention. Outside, hysterical strangers were beating on the glass doors, calling out the names of friends and family.

For the remainder of the afternoon I tried to keep myself busy until the Englishman came out of surgery. I collected dirty bandages, took around drinking water and tried to comfort people in pain. It seemed ridiculous holding hands with a middle-aged man I had never met, trying to tell him that everything was going to be all right, when his intestine was oozing through a gaping bullet hole above his hip. Somewhere this man had a wife and family who had known him all his life and here was I, born on the other side of the world, comforting him as he died.

In the face of adversity people often either break down or become active. Activity provided a buffer. It distanced me from the shock and alleviated the frustration of being powerless. But as darkness began to fall outside and things settled down in the hospital, I began to reflect. The bloodied bandages, which I had been collecting during the day, had been placed in a plastic bag which I'd thrown behind a blue curtain in the foyer. It was not until my last round that something caught my eye.

A black shoe. I knew immediately it was the dead boy's. Hesitantly I pulled back the curtain. There were six bodies in a neat row on the floor, I found myself staring. Six bodies. All of them male, one a Westerner. Who knew what turn of events had led them to where they were when they had been shot? Perhaps, I thought, if the boy had stopped to pick up his shoe when he had lost it, he might be wearing it tonight, sitting at the dinner table telling his mother lies about where he had been all day.

But it was the Westerner who caught my eye. This was reality. The little hole in the side of his neck had ended his life. His body had ceased to be human, no longer capable of action or thought. He was wearing Reeboks. They seemed ridiculous on a dead man.

THE SHUTTERS HAD BEEN CLOSED over the windows. Shafts of sunlight filtered through the slats. I was very tired. It was early morning and the hospital ward was still. The doctors had brought Andrew Reid in about four hours earlier. They had taken his leg off below the knee. He was semiconscious but not, as yet, in any pain. The ward was full of casualties. Relatives had been arriving all night. The woman next to us was sleeping under her son's bed. He had been shot in the eye and she had been awake with him all night.

Beads of sweat formed on Andrew's forehead as the painkillers began to wear off. He started to groan. I didn't know whether it was the anaesthetic or not but he kept saying his foot was itching. I dreaded to think what sort of a job they had done in removing the leg under such conditions.

The itching, and with it the pain, grew gradually worse.

"Ah, Christ, Jon, you must get me some more of that stuff. I'm in agony.' It was the plea of someone in real pain, an undignified guttural whimper. Conscious that it would bring only temporary relief, I asked the nurse to give him some more pethidine.

I needed to get him to the Patan Hospital where they had full facilities. An ambulance proved even more difficult than I had expected. The king had announced a 48-hour curfew and none of the drivers wanted to go out. The Army was patrolling the streets with orders to shoot. I rang the embassy again. They told me the curfew would be lifted for one hour each day at 12 o'clock. They were sending someone to the hospital then and suggested we organise an ambulance to leave while the ban was lifted.

The English are practical in a crisis. The First Secretary from the embassy arrived promptly at 12.15. He was a tall, skinny man with thick eyebrows and grey hair growing from his ears.

'Terribly sorry we took so long to get here, but things are rather unstable at the moment,' he said, leaning over Andrew's bed. 'Anyway, we've done a quick whip round at the embassy and gathered together a few things for you.' He removed a sack from over his shoulder and began to unload it; three packets of Cup-A-Soup, a bottle of orange-flavoured Tang, half a pack of jam biscuits, some magazines, a Somerset Maugham book of short stories, a packet of tea bags and a small bottle of gin.

'Don't know if this stuff will be any good to you, but it was the best we could do. Now, we've contacted your parents and they're okay and we're working on a plane but it may take a couple of days.'

Andrew thanked him very much. I could see he was comforted to have a countryman there. The English have a weird stoicism, inspiring confidence not so much by their actions as by their solid, not to mention stolid, presence.

At 12.30 p.m. the diplomat left and the ambulance driver arrived. We gave Roo (as he had asked me to call him) another shot of pethidine and loaded him onto a stretcher. The lift was broken, so we had to take him down the stairs. Each step brought a wince of pain as the Nepalese porters bumped their way roughly between banisters and walls to the bottom.

Outside, although there was still fifteen minutes of curfew break left, the streets were empty. Roo was loaded into the back of a converted Kombi ambulance. The driver clambered into the front and I into the back. The first road block was 500 metres away. My palms began to sweat and I began to consider the danger of what we were doing.

I peered through the little porthole to where the police stood in a line across the road, their guns levelled at the ambulance. The driver stopped; his hands were shaking. Two men approached and thrust their guns through the window at him. Without warning the back doors were flung open. My stomach dropped and then shot up into my throat. I turned and looked straight in the eye of a gun. For a moment nobody moved. Then, in broken English, the soldier ordered me from the van.

'No,' I said without thinking. 'No, this man must go to a hospital,' I said firmly. Roo groaned. I could see the soldier hesitate. It was all I needed. 'Doctor,' I said fumbling in my money belt for some identification. 'I am a doctor.' I pulled out my driver's licence and gave it to him. He snatched at it, looked at me once and then took it over to his superior. At this stage Roo began to moan. The soldier with my licence returned and handed it back to me. He seemed convinced. He then closed the door and waved us on.

We were stopped six times before we made it to the hospital, which, to my great relief, had an Australian doctor with whom I had no trouble making explanations. They took us in, re-dressed Roo's wounds and then drugged him to sleep. At five o'clock the embassy rang to say they had organised a plane for him the following evening when the curfew was due to be lifted. I had a mug of Roo's gin with soda water, and then, exhausted, I too went to sleep.

It was morning when I woke. Roo in the next bed was still asleep, his round sweaty face motionless. I walked to the window. We were in a large room full of empty beds. I thought of the other hospital foyer and wondered why patients hadn't been brought here.

Outside an eagle perched on a pole. It ruffled its feathers in the wind. Still and resilient, it waited patiently for something to move below. The world belonged to it. All it had to do was wait, eventually it would eat. I looked at Roo lying there with his leg shot off; at myself, lonely and travelling without direction, forcing myself on the world. We had no balance.

The embassy driver came for Roo in a Land Rover. I scribbled his address on a piece of scrap paper and we said our goodbyes. Two years later I would receive a homemade postcard of his artificial leg standing on a pile of rocks overlooking the Khyber Pass.

I took a taxi back into the centre of Kathmandu. The curfew had been lifted. It occurred to me I was three days late for a rendezvous with my friend, photographer Michael May.

I got out of the taxi a few blocks from the hotel where we were to meet. The atmosphere on the streets was still very tense. Only about half the shops were open. Travellers gathered in groups on street corners, each telling their own story of the weekend's events. At intervals along the cobbled roads, little monuments had been set up in honour of those who had been killed; the most poignant being a jumbled pile of shoes.

Inside the hotel gates, visions of the past few days flashed through my head again. The six dead bodies, the boy in hospital, the soldier's gun, Roo's leg. In the foyer a Nepalese pedlar pulled me to one side. 'Hash,' he said, smiling at me through decaying teeth, 'You want good hash, great trip, very cheap.'

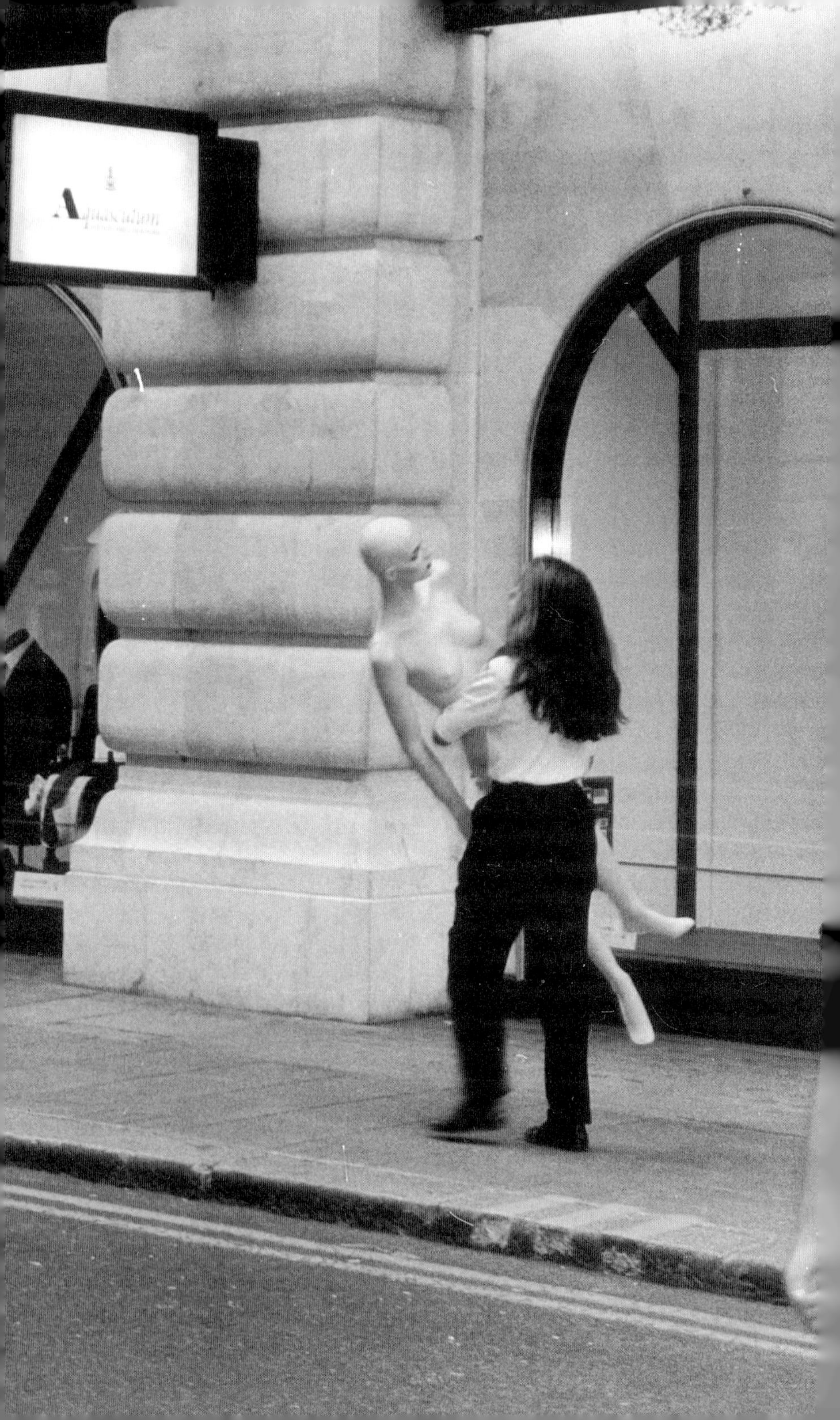

STOP-OVER IN THE FIRST WORLD

England

FROM KATHMANDU I had to fly to London for two weeks to pick up a flight to Africa. The woman next to me on the plane was a window hog. She had her face so close to the Perspex the vibrations made her bun wobble and my first views of England were through the window on the far side. But still it was wonderful. London was square, like an enormous toy train set interspersed with silvery streaks of water. I thought every cricket ground was Lord's and every castle Buckingham Palace. Republican and all as I am, there was something reassuring about arriving in London.

Instinctively, I seemed to know my way around Heathrow. It was comforting to regain my faith in the bureaucracy. Signs actually pointed in the right directions, drinking fountains worked and moving walkways carried your luggage. At Customs the Commonwealth queue moved faster than the others and when I reached the desk I didn't even need to spiel the usual crap to get through. They just stamped my passport and waved me on.

I recognised all the names on the multicoloured Tube map, although being colour-blind made it difficult to work out which line actually went to Earl's Court. 'It's the green one, mate,' said a voice from behind. The attendant directed me to the District line, where I boarded the next train. Sitting with my pack firmly wedged in the overhead rack, I looked down the length of the train at the English reading their papers and listening to Walkmans. I read the advertisements for new cars above the windows and thought back to my last train ride in India. It was an impossible comparison of cultures. I remembered the Indians scrambling their way onto the train at Siliguri; at Earl's Court, a prerecorded voice kept informing the alighting passengers to 'Mind the gap; mind the gap; mind the gap.'

Outside the station gates I was approached by an extremely well groomed drunk, dressed in a thick tweed overcoat. His hair was brushed to one side to cover his bald patch. His beard was long, but neatly trimmed.

'Can I help you sir?' he slurred.

He seemed harmless enough.

'Yeah,' I said, 'I'm looking for somewhere cheap to stay.'

He laughed a little and turned to his three mates who sat along the wall of the station entrance.

'Well, you coul' come'nt stay wiff us,' he gargled, 'But we're a bi' short a room.' His mates laughed and he raised a gloved hand.

'There's places all along here full of Australians. About 12 quid a night.'

'Thanks,' I said, and turned to go.

Before I could get away the drunk grabbed my shoulder.

'You courrn't spare summit coul' you? I'm a bit skint you see.'

'I'm sorry,' I said reaching into my pocket. 'I've only got tens.'

'Sorright son,' he said, excitedly pulling out his wallet. 'I got change.'

The drunk was right. Earl's Court was full of Australians. One of them was my room-mate, George Blake.

'You can call me Oz,' George said, thrusting out a huge hand for me to shake.

'I've been pissed in sixteen countries so far, what about you?'

'Oh, just the one or two, Oz,' I replied. 'I'm a bit of a novice really. But I'd love to go and try a few real English beers.'

'Right,' said Oz, 'I know just the place.' And, pulling on his bright gold Australian rugby jumper, he led me from the room.

I knew relatively little about English beer. Only that they took it seriously and drank it warm. I guessed that if Oz could adapt then so could I. I was looking forward to it. The quaint little English pubs I had seen on TV always seemed inviting. I had visions of men in tweed jackets hunched over pints discussing the weekend sports results, while the portly proprietor stoked his open fire or slowly drew a pint from his brass-handled pump.

The 'Prince of Teck' in central Earl's Court Road, however, was hardly quaint and the two-metre stuffed kangaroo at the end of the bar didn't evoke that 'ye olde England' atmosphere.

'Anyone who's anyone drinks here, mate,' Oz said, striding through the double doors into the cigarette-smoke-filled bar.

There was no sign of David Bowie or Mick Jagger anywhere. In fact, unless anyone who was anyone was called Wayne, Bruce, Charlene, Trudi or Tracey, there was no one who was anyone here at all.

I looked up at Oz, who was about as tall as the kangaroo.

'Great, isn't it?' he said. 'Just like being back home.'

'Yeah. Great, Oz,' I agreed, a little dubiously, but happy nonetheless to be in a familiar environment.

'How about that real English beer then, mate?' I yelled above the noise.

'No worries,' Oz said, leaning over the bar and calling to the barman.

'Hey, Brian: Two Fosters Export when you're ready, thanks, mate.' We drew up a couple of stools. 'Comes in bigger cans,' said Oz by way of explanation.

I SPENT MOST OF MY TWO WEEKS IN LONDON with a girl named Maggie who I met in the hostel where I was staying. We forged an instant friendship. After months of transient relationships and mishaps in the Third World, it was so refreshing to talk to somebody with a common background. I liked her but could not put my finger on why. Perhaps it was because she looked past the boundaries I put up and saw inside.

I felt naked when we talked but still I shared things with her, I never dreamed I'd ever tell anyone. We were kindred spirits, Maggie and I. She alone running from a fragmented world and me alone running from one that was too complete. I felt as if I wanted to share everything with her. Sometimes we sat up until dawn, talking and drinking beers in the hostel lounge room where she buried herself, legs tucked under her, in a large black leather chair, shrouded in blue smoke from her cigarette. I was not in love, I just wanted to know her. When I finally left the hostel, we said goodbye without hugging. It was an awkward moment and as I walked out the hostel door, I felt I had lost something.

It is funny how many people we are acquainted with, but don't really know. I wanted nothing more than to hug Maggie when I left; to say goodbye and to thank her for her friendship. Instead I took the easy option; I chose to stay inside the walls of convention. After a fortnight in which she had been my friend, confessor and confidant, all I could do when I said goodbye was shake hands.

AFRICA

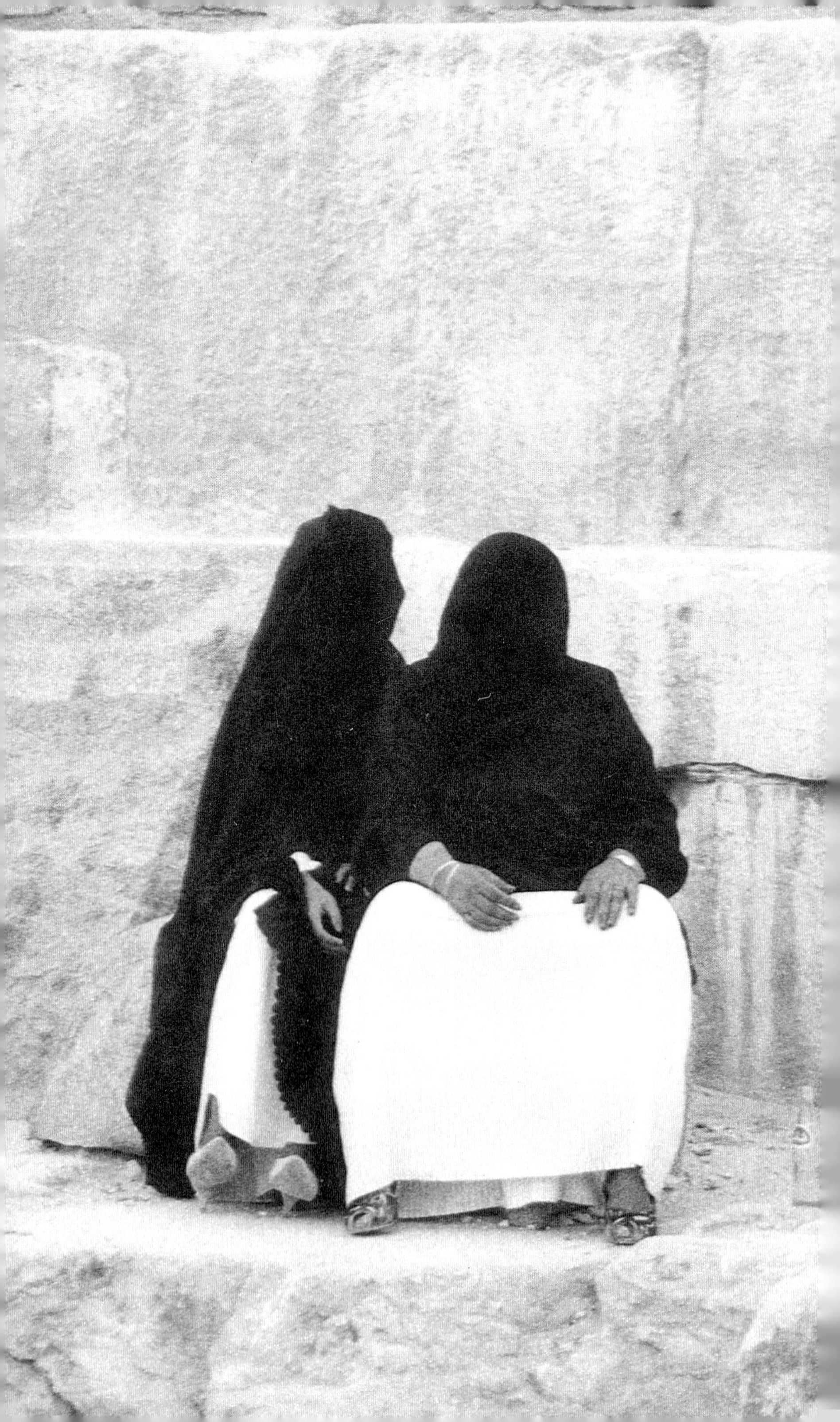

Egypt

THE DESERT HEAT hammered my feet to the ground. Before me the huge, still monuments dwarfed every move I made. Only the souvenir sellers were alive, peddling scarabs and warm drinks where once the pharaohs had walked. I strolled for hours around the pyramids, looking up from different angles; the heat seeping up from the sand, through my shoes, drawing me into the earth. At close quarters it was easy to feel reduced by their massive scale; it's only in the distance they fall into perspective recognisable to a stranger. From even further off, they become harmless silhouettes, just dots in time, pimples on the earth.

Beneath the temple of Cheops, two women, clad from head to foot in black robes, sat chatting on a rock, framed by the contrasting sandstone blocks behind them.. They did not move as I passed them and paused to take a photo. It was 45°, not a breath of wind and even the tourists chose to stay in their air-conditioned buses; only these two women sat in the sun. From a distance, I began to click, taking shots from different angles, when I heard a scream behind me. A man dressed in robes was trotting towards me on a donkey, waving a stick, his curses echoing off the pyramids. I froze, unsure what the problem was. The man came closer and then, leaning forward on his donkey, spat in my face as he passed and moved on to the two women, whom he ushered out of sight.

In shock, I had fallen to the ground, where I now lay with hot spit in my eye. I looked up to where the women had been and saw only the stepped structure of the pyramid, the broad base, the narrowing top rising into the sky.

AT THE ENTRANCE to the Karnac Temple there was a man selling warped postcards. The corners were bent and the pictures faded even though he hid them from the sun in a wooden box. I walked alone, through the temple, past huge pillars covered in hieroglyphics and rows of animal carvings and tablets. I was struck by the immobility; the solidity, so enormous in this country now so poor. It was as though all that had been built and created since was tied to the temples, stagnant and unable to break free.

Where do you go after immortality? Anything more is a burden. Karnac was constructed over generations, each of the Pharaohs trying to outdo his predecessor, the monuments successively bigger and more solid, until eventually there was nowhere left to go. The wind and sand were left to erode away the details of Egypt's attempts to conquer time.

It was a familiar theme in Egypt, the blend between the old and the even older in conflict with the new. In the Valley of the Kings, inside the door of Rameses' tomb, I passed a hawker sitting in the shade of the tunnel entrance. I followed the Pharaoh's story drawn up along the wall. I touched it, as an early explorer might have done, searching for clues. The hawker followed behind me, narrating in Arabic. In the drawings, women carried vases on their heads, snakes rose out of bottles and men in loincloths held rigid poses. I tried to picture the place as it must once have been, thriving with people, digging, working; a passionate place with people as rich and advanced as anywhere in the world. A people who had tried to beat time and become gods on Earth. Momentarily, I was again the explorer I had been in my childhood. The walls came to life for me and industrious noises reverberated up the tunnel until finally we entered the tomb and the emptiness took over again.

A naked light lit the room, I was wearing a T-shirt and shorts from Australia and a crippled hawker was speaking to me in a language I didn't understand – in a tomb built as a meeting place for a dead king and his Gods.

THAT DAY, a letter arrived from my friend Kym in London. I opened it on the way to the boat, to find it contained terrible news of Maggie. Maggie, who had come to London to make a new start and who had sat up with me, philosophising into the night; Maggie whom I had liked but had not loved, who had been special though I hadn't been able to find the words to tell her, had died suddenly of a brain haemorrhage. The words beat inside my head. I kept rereading them over again, trying to make them disappear from the page. On the boat back to Cairo, I rehearsed in my mind the details of her face, the way she had looked away whenever she smiled, the way she had pushed back her hair; the way she had thrust her hands deep into her pockets and walked off up stairs when we had said goodbye. The images were so real, her life so permanent and yet so fragile. Maybe death was nature's way of saying she was still in control; perhaps she is her own memory.

I slept that night in an old wooden *falucca* that creaked as it rocked on the currents of the Nile. Mosquitoes buzzed outside my net and myriad stars dotted the sky. Next to them, the pyramids were nothing. The universe was laughing at the Pharaohs. I thought of Maggie, dead in the physical world but still so real in my mind, and then of the pyramids, thousands of physical hours and years of work, drained, lost and empty in the desert.

Uganda

IN THE TOWN OF KATWE, in western Uganda, two young children looked on as one more passenger climbed on the back of the Toyota utility truck

He was the twenty-sixth. Those of us who had arrived earlier scored the prize seats around the edges, our feet trapped somewhere below in a collection of luggage which ranged from bananas to chickens. The others stood, clinging to each other for support. I sat, self-consciously, as elbows, bums and legs entangled my face in an effort to find room.

With the suspension straining, the utility truck surged forward. A roar of laughter was let out as those standing fell in a heap on top of us. To go through it every day must have been

agonising, but I could not help being caught up in the infectious laughter of people who had learned to accept the ridiculous and live with the extreme.

The journey from Katwe to Kasese was about 40 kilometres, but it was to take six hours. The dirt track along which we travelled had been deeply rutted by the Tanzanian Army when it invaded Uganda in 1979, and we bobbed and bumped our way along the road at an excruciatingly slow pace, stopping now and then to drop people off or pick them up. Bananas, chickens, loads of washing were flung on and off the truck and then either left behind in clouds of dust, or stuffed between someone's legs in an unending display of resourcefulness when it came to finding space.

But still they laughed.

'*Akhuna matata*, no problem,' chuckled one woman as she threw a tied-up chicken into my lap.

'You hold him good *hu*?'

My backside began to ache and I was seriously considering getting off. The 'taxi' suddenly stopped again and the woman with the chicken lifted the animal from me and disappeared deftly over the side in a cackling flash of white feathers. Her place was taken by a striking woman of similar age. She carried a bundle in each arm and, unable to hold on as the ute began to move, she passed one down to me. I accepted it automatically, expecting a bunch of bananas or some such thing, but she had handed me a baby. I looked up at her, and she smiled reassuringly, then turned away, wrapping her scarf around her face against the dust fanning up from beneath the wheels.

I pulled back the cotton sheet to uncover the baby's small, round face. Its pouting lips and chubby cheeks vibrated with each bump, and that peculiar baby smell rose from its freshly washed blankets, triggering in me a protective, paternal feeling.

The child had not yet assumed any signs of the hard life it would lead. Its mother, in contrast, had obviously worked hard for many years. From the side I guessed her to be about twenty-three. Her skin was a deep black and her hair close cropped, presumably to stop nits. With each bump the tendons in her forearm tightened and the muscles in her calves flexed in taut contractions. Her elbows were rough and cracked, her feet flat and broad from the heavy loads she had carried.

Forgetting my pain, I was soon enthralled by the child. It reached up with one little hand and clasped at my beard, the other hand curling its delicate fingers around my shirt collar. I indulged myself by tickling it under the chin. It smiled and giggled, pushing forward its little pink tongue.

Gradually the child began to snuggle itself into my breast with its head and fingers protruding from the blanket. There seemed no better place for it to be and it went comfortably to sleep, allowing me to ride each bump, determined it should not wake.

With each village we passed I gained another picture of the future for this child. Infants played with bottle tops in the dust and herded cows off the street. Some, slightly older, wheeled barrows of corn. In the markets the cycle could be seen to begin again: fifteen-year-old girls carried bananas home, their babies slung precariously across their backs. Childhood in Africa is short.

I wondered if, taken out of this environment, the child would adapt. Given wealth and education, what might it achieve? At this stage of its life it was no different to any other child in the world. In the next six months, it would begin to develop the symptoms associated with inadequate diet and a lack of medical care. It would become part of Africa's vicious, natural cycle which does not discriminate in favour of the weak.

When we arrived in Kasese, the utility truck was more crowded than ever. People began to alight and I was able to stretch my legs. Hesitantly, I rose and scanned the crowd for the child's mother, who had been pushed to the other side in the crush at the near the end of the journey. She was nowhere to be seen.

Disconcerted, I stepped from the vehicle with the baby in one arm and my rucksack across my shoulder.

'Excuse me,' I interrupted a stout woman who had been near me when the mother had boarded.

'Have you seen the mother?' I said, raising the child slightly. 'I think she has forgotten her baby.'

Even as I spoke, the words sounded absurd. Mothers just don't forget babies. The woman looked at me for a moment, then chuckled.

'She not forgot. She hop off two towns past. You mother now.'

At this, the crowd which had gathered broke into hysterical laughter. 'Take it!' they cried.

'Take it! Take it where?' I had been caught completely off guard.

'Take him Entebbe.'

'But the child has a mother,' I protested.

'She gone two town past. You mother now.' The locals laughed again as if to egg the woman on. I was beginning to get a little suspicious. At any moment, I was half expecting a policeman to emerge from the crowd to arrest me for child abduction or some such thing. Whatever the case, I could see I was achieving little by standing there.

'Is there a doctor here?' I asked.

'Where is the doctor?'

At this, various crowd members pointed in different directions. I decided my best bet was the main road and, hitching my rucksack on my back, I set off with the baby.

The doctor's surgery was in a chemist shop next door to the church. There were a number of people in the waiting room when I entered. Hesitantly, I took my place at the end of the queue.

It was more than an hour before the doctor saw me. The child had hardly made a sound, its large brown eyes gazing around the room, focusing occasionally on my face.

I had expected the doctor to be surprised when I entered carrying a black child. Instead he only sighed as he flicked through his notes and listened to my story. I was about to share with him my disbelief that someone could just abandon a child in this manner when he cut me short by raising his finger to his lips.

'In this community everyone must be able to support themselves. I delivered this child six months ago to a girl in the next village. She was only sixteen and had no husband. There were complications during the birth and the mother unfortunately died. The sister, probably the woman you met, has tried to look after it, but, since having another child of her own, she feels she can no longer cope. She has tried once already to give up the child to a group of missionaries who came through here from Kampala two months ago.'

'But why?' I asked. 'Why would she want to get rid of it?'

'She does not want to get rid of it,' replied the doctor, a little angrily. 'She feels she has no choice.' He placed the child on the bench in front of me and, pulling the wrapping from its body, said, 'You see, the child has polio.' The baby's feet were minute and withered. 'She will never walk on those,' he said. 'And if she does not walk, she cannot work and the family cannot afford to feed her,' he added. 'Tonight I will take her back to the village myself.'

And with that, he re-wrapped the baby and placed her back in my arms.

Most of us choose not to think about it. We purge our collective guilt now and then by giving to Band-Aid-like appeals but rarely do we push ourselves to understand. When I say this to people they often take it as a criticism, but it is not meant to be. It is just a fact. Later, after I had left the baby for the doctor to take back, I couldn't sleep. I thought of my own childhood and of the things I had seen in Africa. But no matter how I tried to rationalise the differences, I could not balance the two.

THE RAIN BEAT like little hands on my window. My breath condensed on the glass while the rattle of the ceiling fan above seemed to orchestrate the waiting, as it turned slowly upon its uneven pivot.

It had been a typically hot African day. While the train was moving we had watched the storm blow in over Lake Edward from the Rwanzori Ranges. Eventually it dumped on us, washing away part of the tracks and leaving us stranded.

I wiped the window with my shirt sleeve. Outside, the clouds were clearing. The colours of Africa I had heard so much about began to bounce themselves off the droplets on the window. Passengers had long since alighted and, seemingly impervious to the constant drizzle, had busied themselves preparing dinner.

It was, I surmised, a credit to African practicality and an indictment of Western dependency that I sat there with enough money in my pocket to feed them all, and yet they, with their millet and potatoes, would eat tonight and I would not.

As I looked away from the window I found, to my surprise, that another man had entered the cabin. On leaving Kasese, I had been the only first-class passenger and although the other carriages were full, no one else had ventured into this section. He sat about four seats away from me and, as I had been, was staring out the window. It was difficult to guess his age; his face was deeply furrowed and his eyes an opaque yellow. A large, black hand rested on his chin, his thick nails scratching his greying stubble.

On his head he wore a blue denim cap with the words 'Pepsi-Cola — The Taste of the New Generation', written around the rim. I laughed to myself: nothing seemed more incongruous out here that, on the head of an old man, in a broken-down, bullet-riddled train, which had survived an empire, a dictator and a civil war, I should be reading those words on his hat.

And yet, strangely, it had been a constant on this trip. In the most remote places, where water was not fit to drink, where roofs were little more than banana leaves, where the diet was rice and potatoes, there were the clean, blue, white and red waves of the Pepsi sign.

In a strange way it was comforting. For those of us trying to overstep the bounds of the tourist and actually touch the lives and cultures of Africa, the oppression, whether we are prepared to admit it or not, becomes more and more overbearing. As one passes from village to village in pouring rain or searing heat, on barely navigable roads, one begins to seek out the symbols of the Western world. The naive concept that we can somehow transcend our socialised 'Westernality' and experience Africa is suddenly shattered, when, in the midst of a 'real' African village with a ritual dance taking place in the centre and a thriving barter market on the street next to you, you find yourself staring, somewhat longingly, at a Pepsi sign.

It is not thirst, nor even the colours that attract you. It is the representation of stability, of something familiar and reliable in an intimidating and sometimes hostile environment. It is an escape from reality to the illusion of an Africa that would have us all in soft-top Jeeps, sipping cold drinks and viewing her through double-glazed windows.

How inane it had seemed to read those words: 'The Taste of the New Generation', when, directly underneath, half-naked children with bloated bellies played marbles in the dirt, where entire villages had been hit by AIDS and hospitals were overrun with casualties. Why, I often wondered, when so much was needed in the way of medical supplies, foodstuffs and basic apparel, should the only bastion of the Western world be a Pepsi-Cola sign?

It was, I guess, a credit to the advertisers and yet an indictment of the society that sponsors and rewards them. But then Africa is full of ambiguities, most of them remnants of attempts to tame her. The neon sign, tied by its extension cord to a shop roof with no electricity, is no different from the overgrown rose gardens of the British mansion in Kampala. In retrospect, the 'Coca-Colonisation' has just picked up where a British and the French left off, and the results, it seems, are equally inappropriate.

The carriage door behind me clicked. The old man was gone, and in his place came a boy, carrying a pile of steaming, yellow potatoes wrapped in a banana leaf. I recognised him as a member of the family who had been cooking outside my carriage window. He approached, a little shy at first and then, with a light flicker of his eyes, he slid the food across the table to me and said, 'Here, *Mazoongoo*, eat.'

THE TWO ORDERLIES lifted the emaciated figure, like a dead deer, onto the stretcher. Beneath the metal bed lay the blankets and pots of the family vigil. The hospital had been their home for the past few months. The two children watched as their father was taken from the room while their mother crouched back against the wall and began to sob, a pitiful, guttural wail so desperate I should have been unable to watch. But I did watch, drawn by some grotesque curiosity which feeds off the misfortunes of others, I stared and I did not feel pity, only curiosity and discomfort.

The children's ward smelt strongly of urine. On the beds lay small, embryonic figures, their heads, stuffed with tubes, disproportionately large on top of their bodies. The wide eyes, the feeble hands, the bulging rib cages were the children you see on the news, the ones who bring silence into the living room and then disappear into a McDonald's commercial; the ones you temporarily set out to save with a donation and then forget when the sales are on.

In life it's different. No melancholy background music plays, you see no haunting close-ups, nor do you hear the solemn words of choked-up film stars. Just the normal things happen, normal things that nevertheless seem so incongruous at the time of death. Birds sing in trees, nurses rattle pans, babies cry and flies buzz. It is a fact of life, a continuing phenomenon, not a one-hour, edited, hand-delivered TV special. I was unprepared and found it far more difficult to grasp the living problem than I had when trying to assuage my feelings in front of the television.

Most of the patients were AIDS victims. It is an epidemic in Uganda. In 1988, fifty percent of patients admitted to Kampala Central Hospital were found to be HIV-positive. Most had been unaware. Some did not even know what AIDS was and, of course, almost all were sexually active. Controlling AIDS in Uganda, and indeed in most of Africa, is an uphill battle and it's bound to get worse. While I was in Uganda I never saw a condom for sale. The problem, like many of Africa's, seems insoluble.

It is difficult not to be melodramatic. The hospitals are hopelessly overcrowded, under-staffed, under-equipped. They spend, on average, $US8 a patient, as opposed to an estimated $US80 000 a patient in the United States. In the women's ward, a line of gaunt faces lay swallowed up in their pillows. Some were on beds, others on mattresses on the floor. Relatives often slept nearby, their cooking pots and blankets piled around them.

No one was looking for sympathy; what they needed was understanding and that was something I didn't have. I constantly found myself trying psychologically to sanitise the situation; to turn it into a television documentary, trying to put into perspective their seemingly nonchalant ability to cope with the tragic scenes that faced them every day. I attempted to reconcile what I thought the situation should have been with what it actually was. Every time I reached for some preconceived, media-saturated cliche, I felt I was cheating; as if I were feeling sorry for all the wrong reasons; as if I were laughing at a funeral, a sensory spastic unable to fit the right emotion into the right set of circumstances.

As the queues grew longer outside the patients' post, I searched for candid shots, hoping somehow to capture on film what I had not been able to express to myself. Casually I strolled to a nearby tree. I had always been reluctant to stuff a lens into someone's face. Yet, to get those *National Geographic*-type shots where the face says it all, you have to do it.

At the end of the line there was a girl with a child across her shoulder. She was no older than fifteen or sixteen. Trying not to draw attention to myself, I raised and focused the camera on the child's face. Her nose was running, there was mucus built up in the corner of her eye. It was the perfect shot. I steadied and, just as I clicked, the child looked up and smiled and waved. Embarrassed, I slunk back behind the tree. My stomach fell and suddenly the sensory spastic raised its ugly head again. I was angry. I felt like calling out to her. 'Hey kid, come on, stop that, you're supposed to be dying of AIDS. I'm trying my best to feel sorry for you over here and you get up and start smiling at me.'

I felt as if she had not only ruined my photograph but had cheated me of my 'experience' as well. The kid was not supposed to wave, she was supposed to die in her mother's arms. Isn't that always what happens in Africa?

Some of the dead had been laid for burial behind the AIDS hospital. Looking at a dead body, you suddenly become conscious of your own physical weight on the Earth. Your feet seem to fill your shoes more. You are stuck with an overwhelming feeling of vulnerability and inadequacy when you realise how fragile the human body is. You are looking at limbs which have already begun to swell; bloated like sausages they give off that peculiar putrid smell which reaches inside you, grabs your stomach and turns it upside down.

The two orderlies approached. One was eating a banana. When he finished they began to toss the corpses unceremoniously into a pit.

'Shouldn't you cover them with cloth, or say a prayer or something?' I asked.

'What for?' replied the shorter one. 'They are dead.'

The visit to the AIDS hospital hit me straight in the face. Far from broadening my horizons, it served only to show how boxed-in I was by the euphemisms we use in the West to describe the rest of the world. I could not relate to the real thing. It reminded me of an American tourist I had once seen pay a young girl to look sad, so that he could photograph the real face of poverty in India. At the time I had laughed at him, but in retrospect it was simply a more overt means of doing exactly what I was wanting to do now: force the situation to fit the emotion because it didn't work the other way around.

For years I had lived Africa from the centre pages of the Saturday Extra. *I can remember being shocked when they served food on an Air Ethiopia flight into Addis Ababa. Here I was, off to document the starving millions, and being served a cheese omelette. Where was the poverty and corruption? I didn't even have to bribe an airline official. It makes no sense at all. The Ethiopians could get food to the already well-fed foreigners on their airlines, but not to their starving compatriots on the ground; I could feel anger because a child I'd thought was dying had had the strength to smile and wave while I took its photograph.*

MY FOUR WEEKS IN UGANDA were physically and emotionally difficult. So much of what I saw was unexpected. I saw only a couple of other travellers and so I was looking forward to returning to the relative comfort of the YMCA camping ground in Kampala.

On my arrival I had a shower and washed my clothes. It is one of the great pleasures of travelling to spend a few hours getting clean. I did my washing in a bucket and hung it out on the fence of a concrete basketball court which backed onto the camping ground. My luggage had been greatly reduced over the year and a half I had been away. I was now down to the bare essentials. Every time I stopped for a prolonged stay, I found myself accumulating excess junk. Sentimentally, I would always take it with me when I hit the road again, but within a week it would be gone. I would rip the sleeves off designer shirts, cut the legs off a $90 pair of jeans. On the road the priority became practicality and fashion became a superfluous nuisance.

I often thought of my possessions at home. A whole room full of junk: items for which I had worked and saved for years. A wardrobe full of clothes I never wore, twenty pairs of shoes and only two feet. I felt far more comfortable with my backpack only half full. I loved to be self-sufficient.

I ate with some Italians also staying at the YMCA. They had driven a Land Rover through Ethiopia and the Sudan from Cairo. Initially I had envied them. I was frustrated with the slowness of my progress on foot. The freedom of a car would have saved a lot of headaches. As the night wore on, however, I began to change my mind. From the way they talked it seemed they were more restricted than I. Their route was dictated by the availability of petrol. They had to carry spares of practically everything on the Land Rover. They had all invested so much money in the purchase that they had become protective of it. If it broke down, they did too. Between them, they were transporting over a tonne of materials, almost all unnecessary. I had a few kilograms and I felt equally sufficient.

When we returned to the camping ground it was dark. I was exhausted so I said good night to the Italians, rolled out my sleeping bag and lay beneath my mosquito net. It was one of those rare times when everything was unexpectedly perfect. There was a cool breeze. I was comfortable, a little drunk, the stars filled the sky. On the basketball court a group of girls was singing African hymns. I had seen the girls practising earlier that day, standing in rough formation, dressed in simple pinafores. They had none of the garb of Western girls, none of the pretentiousness of Western performers. Instead they had simple talent, raw and real. They did not try: they just sang a song of Africa. I did not understand the words but the sentiment was clear. It sounded as natural as the wind or rain.

In the morning I woke and ate breakfast. The Italians had already packed and gone. I rolled up my bedding and went to the basketball court to collect my washing, but it was not there.

I asked the supervisor, who said, without emotion, that it had been stolen but that if I was quick enough, I might be able to buy it back at the market.

I stopped at the market on the way to the train. It did not take long to find my clothes, although most had already been sold. There was only a pair of pants and a shirt left. I wasn't angry: such things did not matter to me any more. 'How much?' I asked holding up both the shirt and pants.

'Ten thousand,' replied the man. I laughed and bought them. They had cost me more than eighty dollars in London. It was a bargain to buy them back for two!

DURING MY LAST DAYS in Africa I went to Ngong Hill, where the movie *Out of Africa* was set. I had never read any Isak Dinesen (the pen-name of Karen Blixen) books, but if the movie was any indication of the woman as a writer or a person, I probably should have. I felt we shared an affinity. A self-discovery through solitude, and the discovery of another culture through naivety. Just as I had, she had gone into the world expecting an instantaneous revelation of truth and a spontaneous personal change as dramatic as the environmental one. It was not so. The process is gradual. It is slow and alienating.

Karen Blixen expressed an all-consuming desire to make a mark on the world. I feel the same passion. She wondered whether her colours would be caught in African sunsets, her words sung in African songs. It is a desire to transcend mortality, something for which I think we all struggle.

I was jealous as I left Karen Blixen's house. Rightly or wrongly, I felt she would always be a part of the Africa I sought to know. I, on the other hand, would only ever be a traveller. I passed through looking from behind the glass of my own culture into another whose songs I could never sing. When I am gone no one will know I have been there.

CENTRAL AMERICA

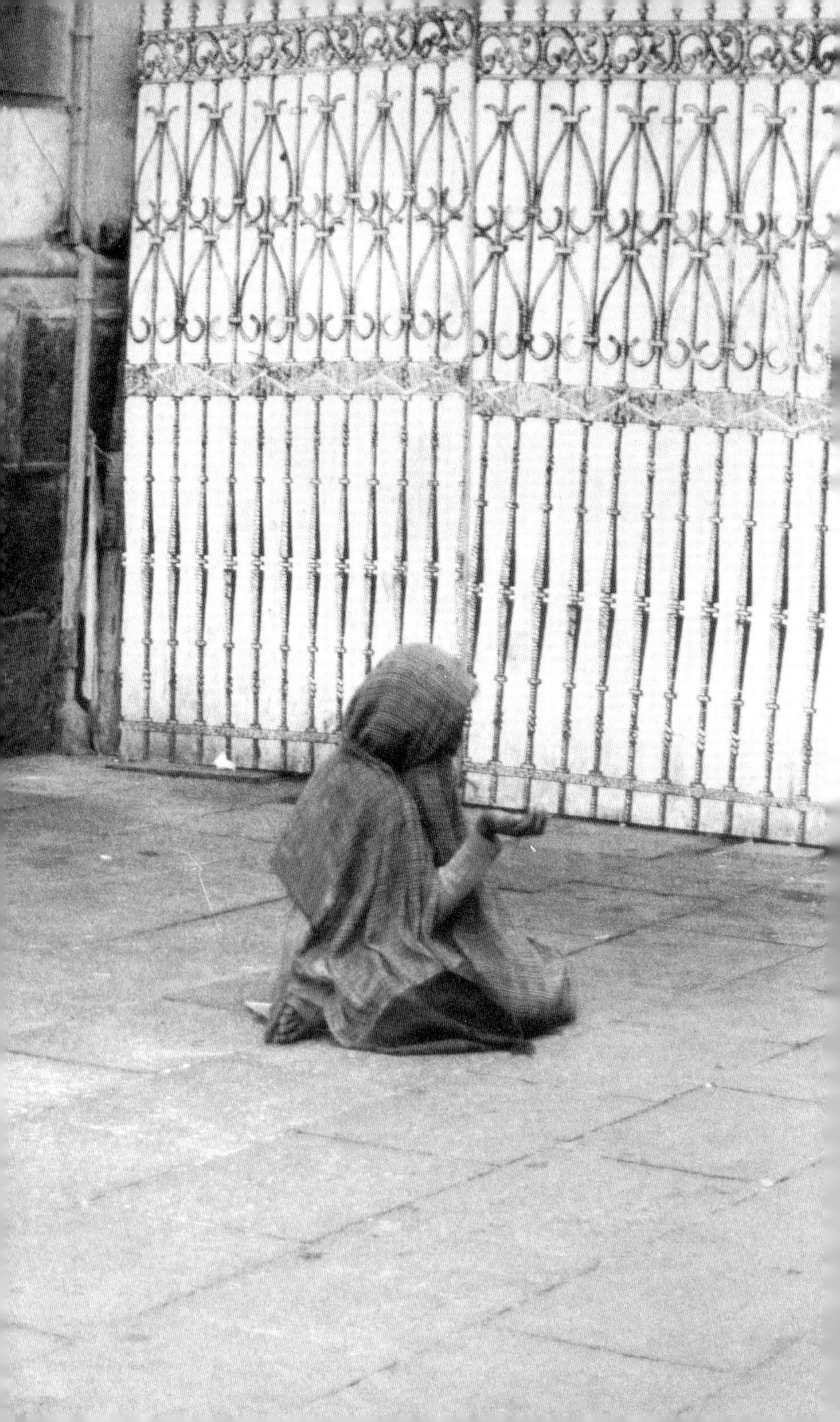

Mexico

MEXICO CITY is like any other major Third World city. It is over-populated, polluted, and disorganised. It is full of people who have lost their spirit, people who seem to exist without purpose, of blank faces and outstretched hands, shifty taxi drivers and run-down hotels. The car exhausts choke you, the piercing noise is constant and you find yourself relentlessly swimming against the tide.

My plane arrived at 1.30 a.m. and there was no bus into town. People walked back and forwards at an exaggerated pace hopping between endless queues. The woman at Information didn't know where the toilet was. As always, someone seemed able to pass straight to the front of the line with no questions asked. The rest sat patiently on their luggage and talked loudly in small groups. Those nearing the ticket desk stared on tiptoes over the shoulders of those in front, waving tickets at the uninterested counter girl. Children played under tables and ran around the knees of adults, while, above it all, incomprehensible messages crackled from the loudspeakers.

Despite this, I fancied the airport was probably the safest place in Mexico City at that hour, so I decided to find a place to sleep. This was not hard as the Mexicans seemed to think that any unused alcove had been designed for this purpose.

I lay down next to two men with no luggage. I guessed they had come in off the street. I padlocked my rucksack, climbed into my sleeping bag and pulled it up over my head.

When I woke some hours later, daylight was dawning outside. Most of those who had been sleeping in the alcoves were gone; only one other man remained. He was lying against the wall on old newspaper with his face covered by a blanket.

I slipped out of my sleeping bag and rolled it into my pack just as two police came around the corner. They did not look at me but walked over to the sleeping man and, without even breaking stride, kicked him in the side. I took my bag and left.

PAINT FLAKED off the ceiling above the hotel bed as I watched. The mattress was hard and flat. Cockroaches roamed the walls and in the bathroom rusty, brown water dripped from the tap.

There was a small television in the corner. I turned it on but the swerving black-and-white picture only exaggerated my isolation. The more I listened to the harsh voice of the Spanish-speaking game-show host the lonelier I felt. Television is the central means of broad communication in any country; to watch it and not understand is to be almost totally alienated. I turned it off and tried to sleep, but was plagued by the blaring of the set next door and the sporadic laughter of my neighbours.

That evening, as I often did in a place new to me, I decided to walk the streets, trying where possible to avoid the main roads. As far as I could see they were full of bridal shops and cafes. I walked for kilometres down cobbled alleys and side streets, past families gathered around the blue lights of televisions, women looking after children, boys pushing water trolleys. Everyone had a place, a purpose. I was an outsider and I felt more alone than ever. The best I could do was watch.

After a couple of hours I came across the central square of Mexico City. At one end was an immense, ornate church, which must once have been an extremely imposing structure; but now, in the half light of dusk, like so much of Mexico City, it seemed to be sinking on its foundations.

Beggars and street hawkers gathered outside. Old women, motionless from sunrise to sunset, kneeled, staring at nothing, their hands outstretched; young girls balanced barefooted infants upon their hips while sinewy boys trundled empty trolleys back to the market. They looked neither sad nor happy, they were just there. It was a day-to-day, hour-to-hour existence.

It was hard to believe that the exquisitely intricate stonework around the cathedral facade was created by the ancestors of the people who now congregated in the streets below it. These people, who had once worshipped pagan gods, now filed into the church thrust upon them by the Spanish. The cathedral interior was immaculate. It was as though passing through the doors were an act of cleansing. There was a haze of incense in the air. At the altar a priest was praying to the packed pews through a loudspeaker. Businessmen sat next to beggars, each in the same pose, each making the same response. Around the edges, smaller groups knelt before lesser altars. Everyone belonged. I wanted to belong.

I sat down next to an old woman and did everything she did. It no longer mattered who she was or what she did, I just wanted to belong with her, to share my solitude. I knelt forward, my hands clasped to my forehead and prayed with an intensity I had not known before, to the God of these people whom I had spent the day pitying even despising. I prayed now that I might join them.

But I felt no relief. No angels sang, nothing touched my soul nor lifted my heart. From the corner of my eye I watched the serene face of the woman next to me; the total relaxation and comfort of this toothless woman who begged from sunrise to sunset. And then I rose and walked back out to the harshness and noise of Mexico City.

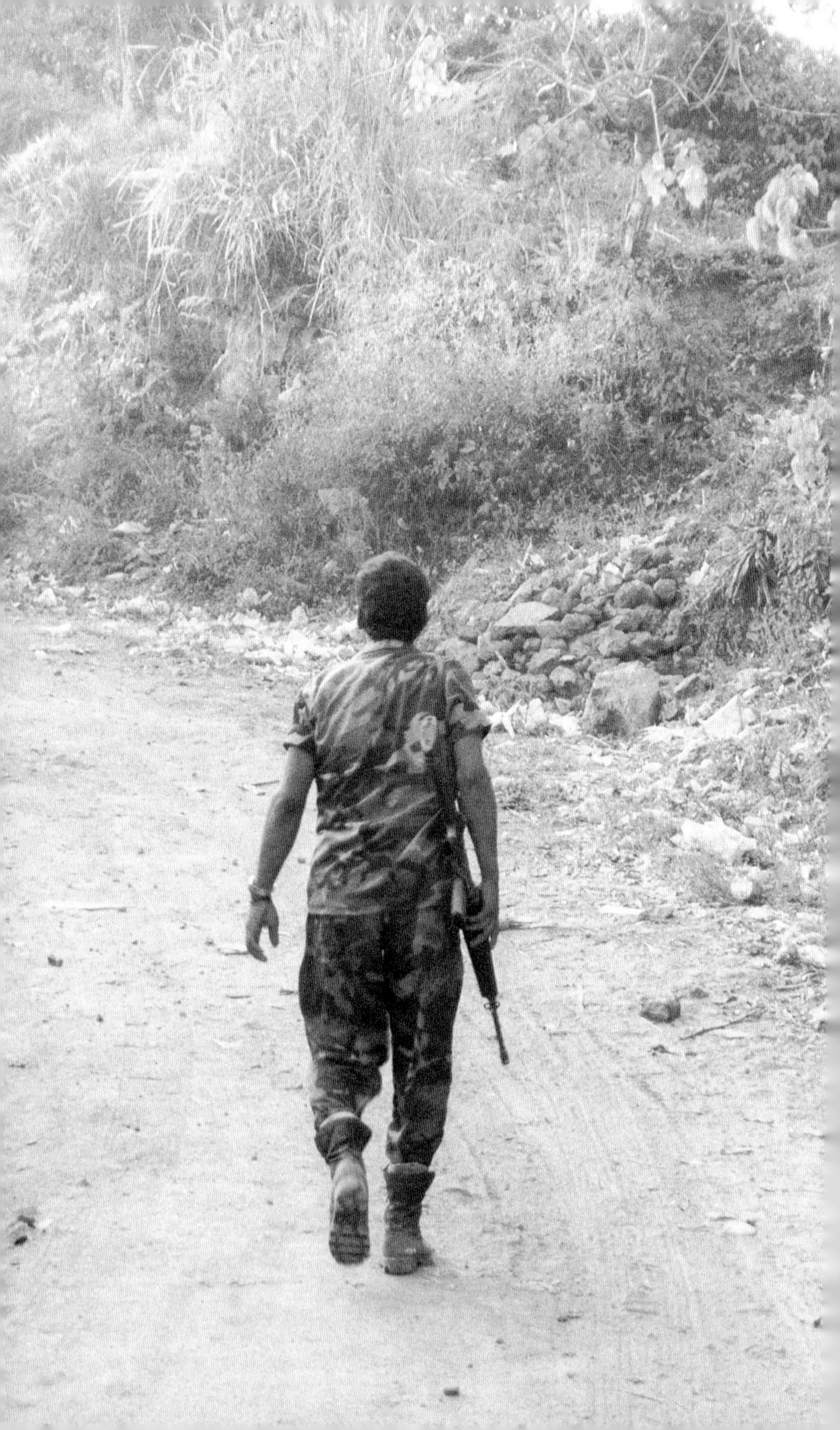

El Salvador

THE ROAD FROM GUATEMALA CITY to San Salvador was like a graveyard. Every eight or so kilometres another cross denoting another death in an accident appeared; the more recent ones draped in strings of flowers, the older ones disappearing behind the tall grass. If you weren't looking for them they could be easily missed.

Men in green Army fatigues, with machine-guns across their laps, sat at checkpoints along the road, between the crosses. They did not smile. They pointed to the luggage compartment, which the bus conductor opened, and they prodded around underneath for a while before waving us on.

At the border everyone was forced to leave the bus and stand next to their luggage as it was unloaded. The soldiers were silent, making their commands with gestures from their guns.

The Customs officer eyed my passport suspiciously.

'Why you want to go El Salvador for?' he asked accusingly.

It was an obvious question and yet I was stumped. I couldn't really tell the truth: 'Oh, you know, I just wanted to see the country where 75 000 people have been murdered in the past ten years. Maybe talk to a few FMLN guerrillas, take a few photographs, you know the kind of thing.'

I opted instead for what seemed a ridiculous answer: 'Just tourism,' I said.

The officer stared up at me for an uncomfortably long time. Then, with a disgruntled scowl, he stamped my passport and thrust it back across the counter.

Our arrival in San Salvador was marked by a military buildup. The bus had entered the city a long way from the centre. Most corners were barricaded with sandbags. Houses were surrounded by barbed wire and high walls. The traffic was light and heavily armed guards patrolled most buildings.

Only a week earlier in Mexico City, I had seen some film from El Salvador showing a man being gunned down as he tried to run across a main road. I could not understand the words, nor did I know if the clip was recent, but the pictures of the butchered bodies which had followed this had certainly made me think twice about visiting.

The bus station and surrounding streets were dimly lit and disconcertingly empty. Judging by the houses, I had stumbled upon the wealthy side of San Salvador, and the haste with which the other passengers alighted and then disappeared made me wonder how safe the area was at this time of night. The juxtaposition between what I had seen on the way in and what confronted me now was unnerving; TV cameras, guard dogs, electric fences and barbed wire were everywhere. I walked up the street, conscious of my own footsteps, catching glimpses of the huge houses behind the iron gates. The apparent wealth was not the El Salvador I had expected and although there were no signs of danger, I felt uncomfortable and isolated.

On reaching the main road my spirits were lifted by brighter lights and familiar signs heralding a Pizza Hut restaurant, which, although manned by an armed guard, was the most familiar thing I had seen since leaving the United States.

Unsure which way to go, I was unfolding my map when I heard shouting from a group of men across the street. When I looked up one of them was making his way towards me. There was little traffic, and before I had time to react, the man was at my side.

'Welcome to San Salvador,' he said, smiling. 'I am Carlos.' He thrust out a hand for me to shake. 'It is not good to be on the street here at this time. Let me take you downtown. There you can find many hotel.'

There are times when travelling when you have to break the rules and go with your instincts. Something told me I should trust Carlos. And, at that stage, the thought of being mugged downtown was almost preferable to the thought of standing alone where I was.

The 101 bus took us along Escalon Avenue and into the centre of San Salvador. The streets and the bus became gradually more crowded, until eventually there was hardly room to move. From the window I watched as the footpaths first filled, then overflowed with people. The roads, too, filled with cars and familiar Third World smells wafted in on humid clouds of black smoke from passing buses. Carlos smiled reassuringly, but the further we drove into the mire of flashing lights and honking horns, the more trapped I felt.

The bus stopped and Carlos grabbed my hand as we pushed our way out through the rear door.

'San Salvador,' he pronounced, proudly gesturing with an outstretched arm.

We had come to a brightly lit central plaza, filled with hawkers. The cries of yelling vendors punctuated the distorted blaring of tape decks mounted on the different stalls. The vibrancy was something I had not expected in this city, that had for so long been under the shadow of death.

'What kind of hotel you like?' asked Carlos.

'Cheap,' I replied and he led the way.

The hotel was about ten minutes away, down a small and relatively deserted alley. The San Salvador I had expected began to emerge, the noise slowly abating with each corner. The gutters were filled with fruit peelings and plastic bags, beggars squatted in rows against the crumbling walls and the blackened feet of those trying to sleep protruded onto the street. Most of the lights had gone out and although it was dark I could make out the hollow windows and empty shells of earthquake-ravaged buildings. Men walked in twos and threes between dimly lit bars. We turned down a lane and I was beginning to wish I had not used the word 'cheap', expecting at any minute that someone, even Carlos himself, would pull a knife on me.

The Hotel San Pedro turned out to be nice. Carlos booked me a room for $5 a night and I asked him to join me for a drink in the bar. I was keen to talk to someone about life in El Salvador to see if what we had heard in the West was true. Carlos, however, was reluctant to talk about the war and tried to tell me instead of the natural beauty of the place.

'We get so few visitors here that I enjoy the chance to show off the beauty of my country. I will write for you the places you must visit. If I were not working, I would take you there myself but I have my family to support.'

Carlos wrote me a list of places I should visit and how to reach each of them. We talked a little longer. I thanked him for his help and offered him money for a taxi home, but he would not accept it.

The following morning was hot and, being a Saturday, the streets were again crowded. I made my way back to the market square, where I walked for hours up and down the rows of stalls, watching the faces and wondering what stories lay behind them. I studied the soldiers, boys mostly, as they stood about, some staring coldly at passers-by, others leaning lazily over their guns.

A shanty-town, which backed onto one of many military bases in the area, sprawled in a valley about six blocks from the square. Dozens of townships like this had sprung up after the earthquake in 1986 and most of them were still there. It was a maze of alleys littered with household rubbish. Most of the houses were built from planks of wood, cardboard or corrugated iron. The roofs were held down with worn-out tyres and stones. A river separated the town from the Army base, the banks dotted with women doing their washing. A little further upstream, others used it as a toilet.

I picked my way down the embankment where large numbers of scrawny chickens and skinny, diseased dogs ran about between coconut husks and plastic bags. When I had reached the bottom, I sat for a while, watching a group of women washing, twisting long cotton sheets between them, then beating the excess water out on the rocks. They did not seem bothered by my presence until I produced my camera and began to discreetly take photographs. I had taken about three before one of the women noticed. Her reaction was instant. Muttering some words and looking nervously over her shoulder as she ran, the woman left her washing and led the others frantically up the hill. It took me a second before I realised what had happened and I turned towards the walls of the Army base. From the two turrets on either side, about ten metres above, guns were levelled straight at me. I froze, uncertain what to do. The whole area had suddenly gone quiet. 'No photograph, no photograph,' one of the soldiers yelled. I lifted my camera slowly for them to see, and, opening the back, I allowed the film to fall out. There was no reaction from the soldiers. I stood, unable to move. 'Vamoose,' yelled one of the men, and, slowly, with the women's washing floating away downstream behind me, I made my way back up the hill.

When I returned that night to the hotel, I found Carlos waiting for me in the bar. He was eager to hear how much I had enjoyed the tour he had planned for me.

'Sit down my friend,' he said, ordering two beers. 'So, did you see the volcanoes and the lakes? Aren't they magnificent?'

'Well, actually Carlos,' I replied, embarrassed, 'I spent the day in the shantytown near the military base. I was stupid. I tried to take photographs without thinking.'

The smile disappeared from Carlos's face. He looked cold.

'And now I suppose you have seen the El Salvador you were looking for?' he said. 'Yesterday I offered you a chance to see a real El Salvador, my El Salvador, but instead you go looking for the El Salvador you want to see. Well if that is what you want I shall give it to you. Now sit and listen,' he ordered in a bitter tone.

Caught between humility and surprise I obeyed.

'My father was an educated man and an outspoken supporter of land reform in El Salvador,' Carlos began. 'He often wrote articles for the newspapers even though he knew the possible consequences. You see, he loved this country. In 1982 the *esquadrones de muetre* discovered his name. They came to our house in the night. Five men. My mother and father they tied on their bed and me they tied to a chair in front.' Carlos looked me straight in the eye. I could see he wanted to hurt me with what he was about to say. 'They then slit my father's throat, gagged my mother and stabbed her through the breast. 'Tell everyone,' they said, and then they left me there to watch them both bleed to death.'

Carlos sat back on his chair and took a swig from his beer. He wiped his mouth with the back of his wrist and looked at me again.

'So, now I am telling everyone,' he said.

'I'm so sorry Carlos,' I said pathetically. 'I had no idea.'

Carlos just nodded and then softened his tone.

'Now, wouldn't you rather I told you a tale about how as a young boy I used to chase yellow butterflies among the flowers by the lake? You see, friend, that too is a story of El Salvador.'

IT TOOK SIX HOURS to make the 45-minute trip to Lake Ilopango. The first bus had taken me in the wrong direction, the driver assuring me the whole way we were heading for Ilopango. Instead I waited in a dusty little town outside Santa Tecla for two hours for the next bus. When I boarded, the same driver was driving.

'Ilopango, Ilopango,' he said laughing. The trip took another three hours.

The bus stopped at the top of the road and the driver gestured, 'Ilopango.' There was about an hour of daylight left as I followed my shadow across the road, kicking up puffs of dust with each step.

At the end of the road, the lake came slowly into view. For an hour I perched halfway up the mountain, looking at the lake and the volcanoes behind it. Birds twittered and flew in bunches, while colourful insects hovered around the flowers.

To the local people this valley was water, fish, farm land, and probably the only land they knew. I wondered if they thought the whole world was like this. To an FMLN guerrilla this would be home too, but a home of a different kind: one which could bring life and death, one where the jungle was both friend and enemy. To the pre-colonial Indians, the lake was the home of the gods, a sacred place. Every year Indian priests would drown four virgins in sacrifice to their gods. I wondered if, when being led down to the shore, a virgin had ever stopped to listen to the birds or look at the insects.

THERE IS A STILLNESS in the air. I am at home on this bus, my sweat-drenched back sliding on the vinyl seat. Most people are silent. Two women talk quietly in the back; their conversation rolls on the humid air.

I was reminded of schoolboy trips in the bush in Australia, to hot, deserted country towns where dogs sleep on street corners. I stared at the old, round, three-spoked steering wheel and the cracked windscreen and let my mind wander to the backyard of a house I remembered from my childhood, where a rusted Holden sat on bricks, behind long grass. Wires dangled from the dash. There was a hole in the floor and spider webs in all the corners. I was four years old, driving the car, straining to see out the window while my little hands struggle across the decrepit steering wheel. And then a child began to cry. The bus started, and I was back in El Salvador.

It was an hour's ride to the top of the volcano with the bus grinding and dipping its way up the hill. The driver hardly watched the road, in conversation with his conductor. The woman in front of me picked nits out of her daughter's hair. Beside me, another wrapped a scarf around her face and head to block the dust. It was like sitting next to the invisible man. I don't know what I expected to find at the top. Perhaps a view or a little village to explore. On arrival however, I discovered the trees had blocked the view and all that remained at the top of the mountain was a little shop. Disappointed, I bought a warm Coke and began the long walk back down.

I watched the villagers carrying home their goods from the market; women with huge bundles of sticks or jugs of water on their heads; children with sacks of grain or coffee. I wondered why they didn't catch the bus.

The woman in front of me lost her footing and the sticks she was carrying fell off her head. She laughed and we picked them up together. She tied the sticks back into a bundle and motioned for me to lift it for her. It was heavy and I could barely shift it so she stooped beneath the bundle to help me.

'Here,' I said in Spanish, offering her a little money. 'Why don't you take the bus?'

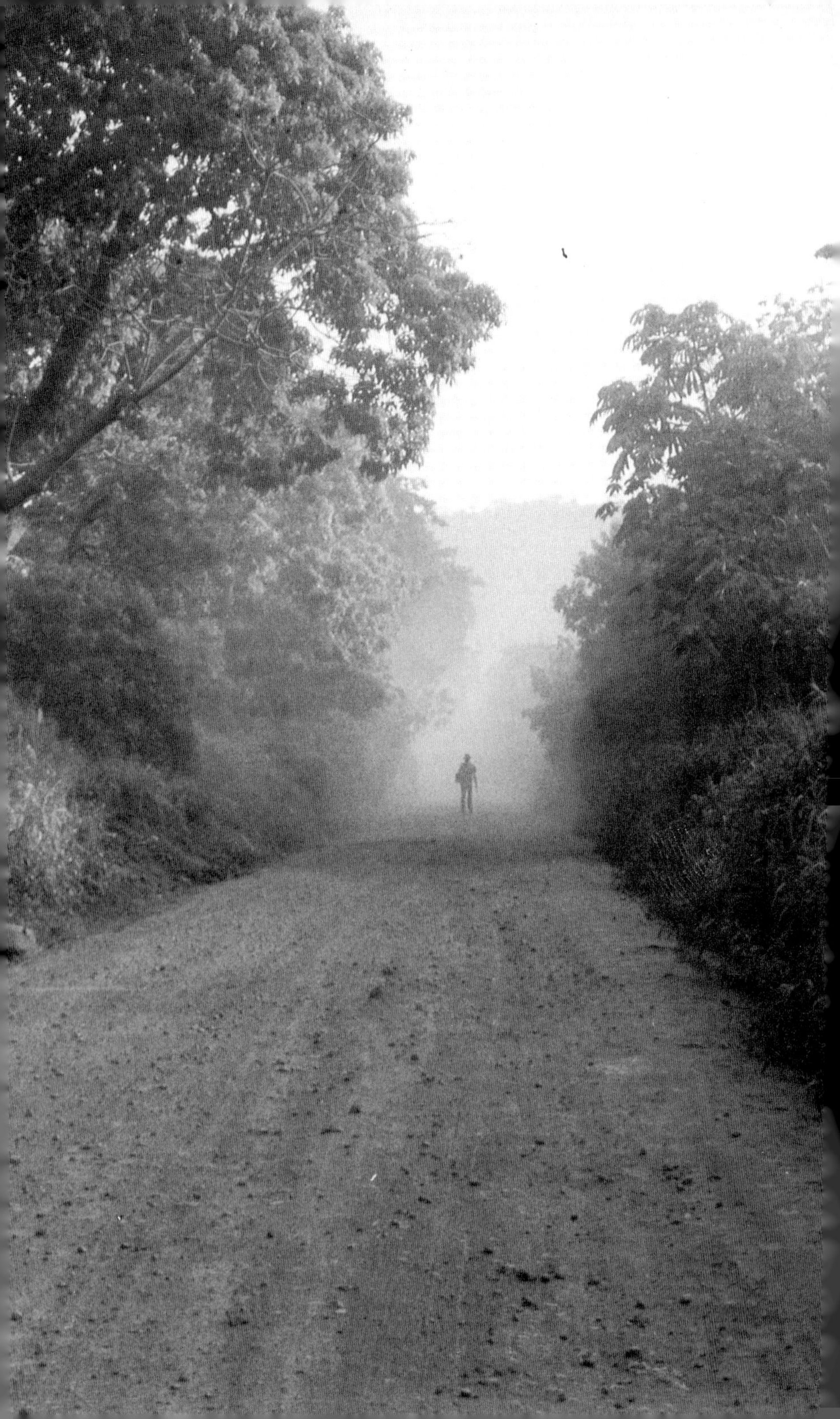

'No thank you,' she replied. 'But I will have the money.' She took the coins and walked on.

The road was full of people going about their business and I decided to stop and take a photo. As I did so I heard yelling and looked up to see a group of children come running down the dusty road behind me. When I turned back the old woman and everyone else on the road had disappeared. As the children neared, they kept looking backwards, until they ran past me and dived into the jungle on the side of the road.

'Gringo, gringo,' called the youngest boy, urgently motioning for me to join them.

'*Pronto, aqui.*'

As I ran into the bush two shots like the magnified crack of ice cubes hitting warm water echoed up the road. A man appeared at the crest of the hill, his gun cocked at his waist. We watched in fear from the bushes. This can't be happening, I thought. There were two more shots and then the man was gone.

We waited. For at least a minute nobody moved until, hesitantly, people emerged from the jungle, checking occasionally over their shoulders as they scurried back along the road.

I had no idea why all this had happened. I could only suppose someone had not paid a tax to the guerrillas. The kid who had been hiding next to me introduced himself. His name was Juan and he proudly announced to me that he was eight years old.

'Be careful of the guns, gringo,' he told me as he stood up to walk away. I gave the kid a buck and watched him dart onto the road. I tried to do the same, but my legs were shaking too much.

IT WAS SUNDAY and the people of San Salvador had dressed in their finest clothes to go to church. Despite the barbed wire and armed soldiers, the mood inside was happy. Colourfully dressed families talked in groups to one another. Young girls giggled in pairs as they eyed the young men who, in return, feigned indifference. Drinks and food were served in a large shaded area at the back and the cool breeze which blew through the courtyard offered welcome relief from the midday heat.

Inside the church a local band was singing up-beat songs of praise as a young soldier entered the door. Nobody seemed to notice. I shifted rather nervously as the soldier, slowly opening and closing his fingers around the trigger of his gun, scanned the crowd. The tempo of the music picked up. The people began to clap.

The soldier took two steps forward, the sun glinting off the back of his black helmet. He raised the gun and I rose from my seat, about to move behind the pew for protection, when he slung the gun off his shoulder, placed it against the wall and, dipping his hand in the holy water, dropped onto one knee and began to pray.

PANCHILLMALCO is a little Indian village about sixteen kilometres from San Salvador. The first thing I saw was a pig trotting across the road and into the gate of a house as if it owned the place. I liked the look of this town.

I considered not getting off the bus at all. Camera-toting visitors change places like this. At first they are a novelty. Then it's a living and finally the locals depend upon the tourist. I don't know if it is right or wrong to consume someone else's culture in order to satisfy a longing of my own. I only know that sometimes, when I ask to photograph someone, I get such a look of anger, I cannot deny that what I, and many other curious people, like me, are doing is changing lives for the worse. Even so, I got off the bus.

The cobbled central street ran the length of the town. Girls carried water on their heads in plastic jugs, boys carried bags of soil or wood on their backs. Chickens, dogs and pigs roamed around homes and in the streets. They lived and ate and, in turn, were killed and eaten.

Children began to gather around me. Most just looked, some asked for money, others wanted to be photographed.

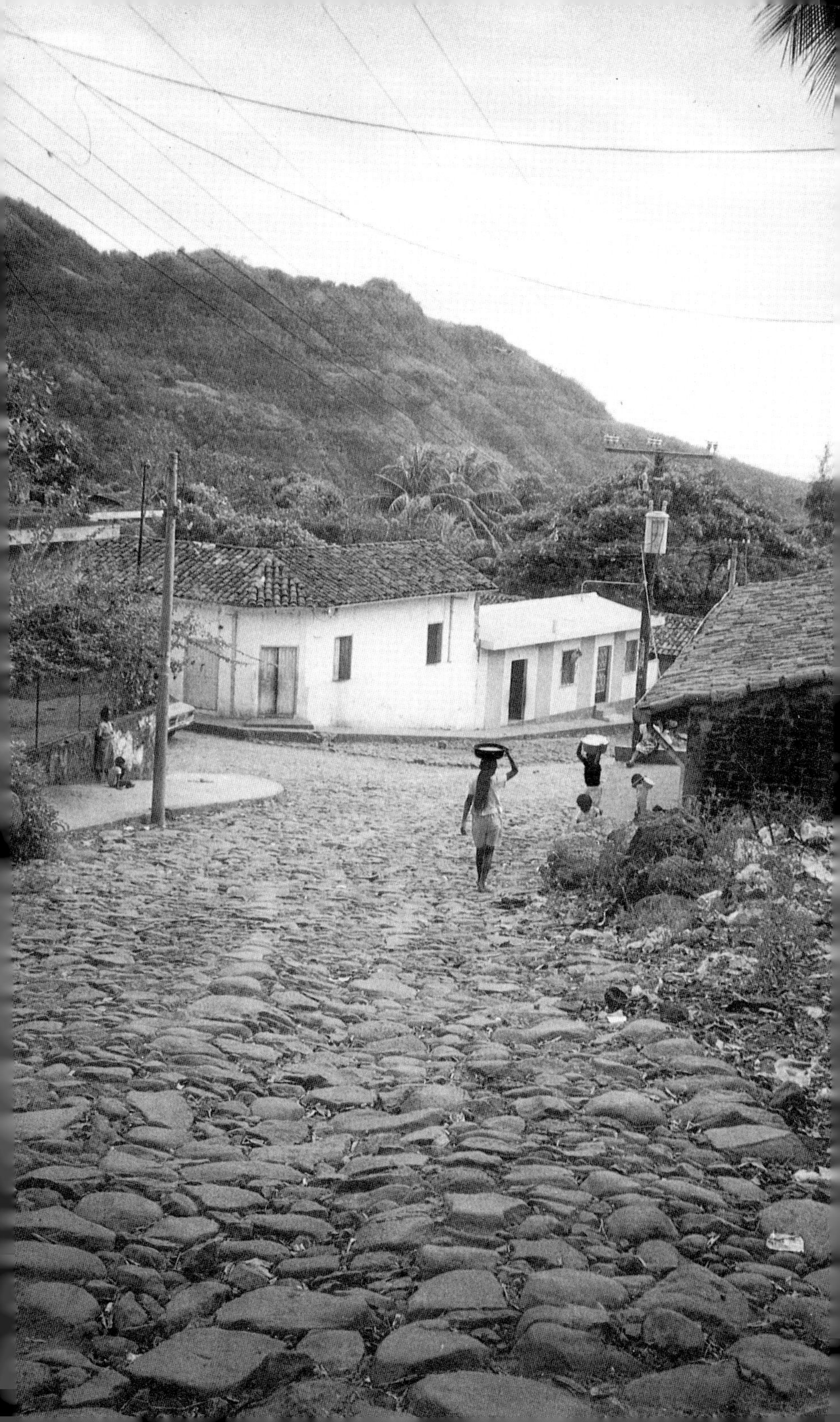

A family was selling pottery jugs, about fifty of them, all made by hand and all roughly the same. Or at least that is the way it first appeared until I noticed an old woman running her hand meticulously around the inside of a pot. Three hours later, she would still be there making her final decision. It was probably the biggest purchase she would make that month.

At the end of the road the town finished and opened up into a valley. Carlos was right when he told me there was more to El Salvador than the civil war we saw on TV.

I walked on into the valley until the children following stopped abruptly and would go no further. I headed into the jungle, watching the yellow and blue butterflies as they flew in circles around each other. Small multi-coloured birds fanned their delicate tails and wild-flowers dotted the greenness.

The jungle thinned and my path opened onto a hillside graveyard. As far as I could see, randomly placed blue and white crosses speckled the tall grass. Hundreds of them rolled down into the valley. I was struck by its informality. This graveyard had been here for longer than the fifteen years I had known of the troubles in El Salvador. It had seen the fall of the Mayans, the slaughter of the Spanish conquistadors, the horror of the twentieth century death squads. Perhaps it was the centuries of dying that made it so peaceful.

I thought when I began travelling that time would mean nothing, but it was always there. There was always a bus to catch, a bill to pay, or a friend to meet. Sometimes, when waiting for a bus or an aeroplane, I would look at my watch. It seemed strange that this was the same watch I had used before leaving Australia to check how much longer my classes had to run before the bell rang; the same watch that had counted the hours of my sickness in India and marked the minutes it had taken for a man die in Uganda. Some days I became so bored, I resorted to studying the minutes by counting the number of times the second hand passed 12. Other times I went for days without looking at my watch.

Until the age of three, I think I did live outside time, spending my days consumed in whatever was taking place; eating whenever

I was hungry and not at lunch or dinner time; playing when I was bored and not at playtime. I tried hard to recapture the feeling on my travels but inevitably I found myself planning dates ahead in my diary and running late for trains.

My third Christmas just seemed to happen. Food, presents, and family. My mother gave me plastic spacemen but from then on life became a series of time frames. I was always waiting for something: to go to school; to get out of school; to go on holidays; for school to begin again. The night before my fourth Christmas my cousin Sarah and I were so excited we went to bed at four in the afternoon, so the morning would come more quickly. We had became victims of time.

Somewhere in the process of learning to live by time the quality of life is degraded. Unlike children we don't do things because we want to, we do them because it's time to do them.

That morning when I woke in San Salvador, I was worried. I was still tired but if I was to catch the bus to Honduras, it was time to get up. I was about to get out of bed when I asked myself, 'Why? You're tired. When you're tired you sleep,' and so I slept. A long deep sleep. It was one of the few occasions on my travels when I felt that nothing mattered.

Many travellers are concerned to show disdain for time. They will try to answer any question vaguely, as though they never think about it. But always in the back of their waist pouch is a ticket home, or the money to buy one. It is comforting but it also means we can never know what it is to endure a place. To know Australia has always been 48 hours away has got me through a lot. There have been only a few times when I have been trapped and unable to leave. They scared me. I felt out of control and suddenly I found myself panicking, longing for the order of time.

I once met a bloke from England who told me he had a great time in Australia. He talked about a visit to Uluru (Ayers Rock) and crossing the Harbour Bridge and I thought of endless, hot, summer days at the local baths; cricket between two rubbish bins in a suburban street at dusk; never-ending drives to Brisbane and rainy days in Melbourne.

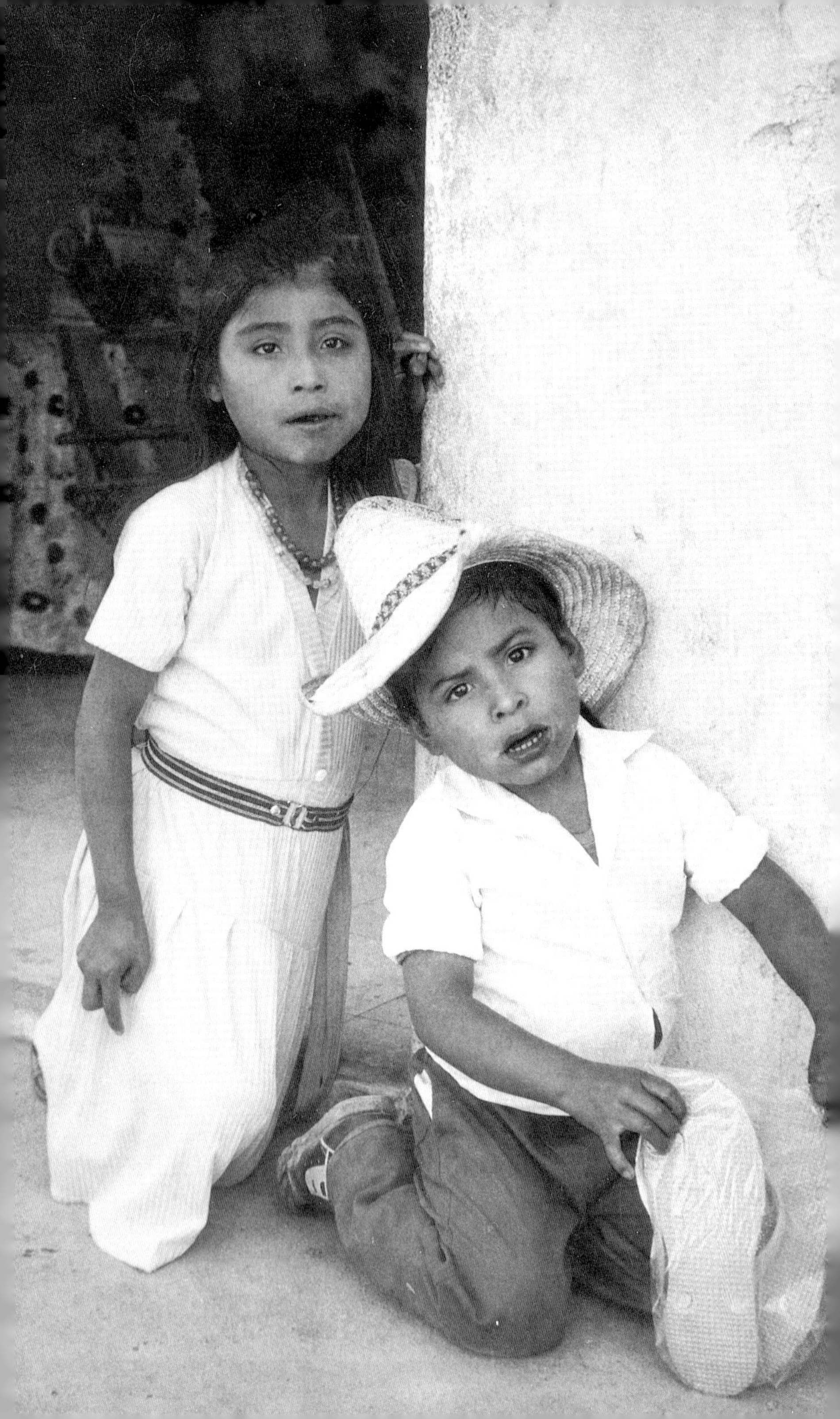

Honduras

NUEVA OCOTEPEQUE was like any of a million hick towns I had visited these past two years. For every day I spent looking at the Taj Mahal or Mount Kilimanjaro, I spent six in places like this. Chickens scratched around in the dirt, boys ringing bells wheeled cartloads of wood while I sat drinking the inevitable warm Coke and waited for a bus.

A man rode into the bus station on his horse. Hondurans make good cowboys but the horses are scrawny, dispirited beasts with sagging backs.

The cowboy dismounted and tied his horse to a pole, then strolled over to the drinks cart. He searched his pockets for money, but didn't seem to have any. He looked thirsty, so I decided to buy him a drink.

'*Dos* Coke,' I said to the man.

The cowboy was obliged.

'I have just a little English but thank you,' he said. 'We can talk a little then I must go.' We sat in the shade and sipped our Cokes.

'What do you do?' I asked him.

'I drive cattle,' he said.

'All your life?'

'Since I was five,' he sighed. 'But it is no more the same. The trucks have come now. The cowboy is finished.'

'Do you make much money?' I asked.

'I don't know,' he replied, forlornly.

The sun had hardened the cracks in the corners of his eyes which squinted from beneath the rim of his weather-beaten old hat.

'I must go,' he said, finishing his drink.

I wanted to ask him why he seemed so sad, but I didn't. Instead I asked, 'If you could have anything, senor, what would it be?'

He looked at me, sheepishly, and then pointed to his top lip from which grew a few, scraggly, grey hairs.

'I wish I could have a moustache,' he said nodding his head. 'In Honduras a man is not a man without a moustache.'

THE DETAIL OF THE SKULL carved into the stone was simple but precise; the face grotesque, but alluring. I was surrounded by jungle and it was early morning, but I could tell already the day would be hot. In the cool of the shade, I could smell gum leaves and I watched as yellow butterflies fluttered between the rocks, seemingly bouncing off the jungle noises: larking birds and howling monkeys.

Ahead was a pyramid. The stones were crumbling and large trees protruded from its side, their roots spreading like serpents across the rocks. Like the pyramids of Egypt, one could still sense their grandeur and yet, as always, I was made aware of man's failing quest for immortality.

To my left and right were similar pyramids, slightly less grand. I closed my eyes and tried to go back one and a half thousand years, to the height of the Mayan civilisation. I knew little of the Mayan culture but it was not hard to imagine the colourfully dressed, black-haired Indians roaming these walls, the jungle alive around them.

On top of the pyramid emerges a god; a man in robes, and there is silence. People stare. Then the victims, perhaps enemy warriors or virgins, overwhelmed, perhaps paralysed with fear, appear. There is fire, the priest begins to chant, raising his arms. The vanquished are tied crucifix-like beside him and with a knife he splits their chests and removes their hearts with his hands, lifting them above his head. The gods and the people are pleased. The victims are then rolled down the stairs to a pool of crocodiles, who eat the remains. Somehow violence is transcended and the scene appears spiritual rather than barbaric.

The hand that carved the stone faces around me understood what happened here. He has used perhaps only six lines to create his image and yet it completely captures the atmosphere, the coexistence of life and death, heaven and earth that seems to pervade this place.

Beneath the ground, in the amphitheatre, lie the bodies of Mayan kings. They and their spirits are still here, peaceful. They have grown up through the trees that have taken root on the walls and they watch, from a new cycle of disguise, over their kingdom as they have done since 500 AD. A lizard crawls on the rocks, pausing cautiously; fleetingly there is life, and then it disappears into a crack.

Slowly, gracefully, as an old man ages, the jungle is taking over. The roots of trees are raised from the ground, rocks wedged in their forked trunks. Birds have made their nests in the altars and flies buzz. A vine has begun to grow around the foot of a statue. Perhaps someone will cut it, perhaps not; eventually the fallen leaves, the grass, the trees will cover the faces which have stared for fifteen centuries upon the surrounding stones; but the faces will always be there.

There is a stone pillar carved with reptiles, and men with

helmets, and ugly, dragon-like faces. Every centimetre has symbolic motifs. They represent a culture of a people and a time I can never know. In front of me are the questions and answers I seek but I cannot see them. I lean across and touch them, as I have tried to do many times before on this journey. I run my fingers along the curves that were cut with intent and knowledge by the maker; but I touch only stone.

IN THE DUSTY TOWN OF FLORIDA, on the Guatemalan border, the Hondurans wore the high-peaked, low-browed hats peculiar to the region. Some carried machetes, a kind of status symbol among men, others sipped beers on the steps of the bar. Everybody stood in the shade, not bothering to move, legs crossed, hands on hips. A man rode past and in the distance a rooster crowed.

There were only four buildings in the town and three of them were closed. Behind the counter of the open one sat an old man fanning himself in the shade.

'What do you sell?' I asked him.

He looked up slowly.

'Beer,' he replied. 'Beer and hats.'

'I'll take a beer then,' I said.

He sat forward and lifted the lid of the ice chest.

'Sorry,' he said, closing the lid again and sitting down in his chair. 'But we are all out of beer.'

ON THE BUS to Tegucigalpa I began to feel ill. First my stomach constricted and then came the hot and cold flushes I had felt in India. I was scared. I would be going home soon and I could not bear the thought of a bout of dysentery before then.

One by one the familiar signs returned. I began to notice the pot-holes, each bump harder to take. I loosened my jeans. The sweat began to pour down my arms and neck. The pains in my stomach became so intense I had to sit doubled over. Again, as in India, my surroundings became insignificant and the drudgery of Third World-living closed in around me. Time stopped. If I could only click my fingers and be back home, I thought. Why did I do this to myself? Gradually I became aware of things I had not noticed since India. My seat was too small, petrol fumes rose through the floor, fat women thrust their backsides in my face and their elbows in my ear. Children talked in piercing, loud voices, vendors pushed rotten food and warm Cokes in my face. Cigarette fumes and body odour filled the air and the constant, distorted sounds of Spanish songs blasted through the bus speakers.

My world turned in on itself. I clutched my stomach, raising my knees to my chest. Briefly the pain passed, but I knew I had to get off the bus. I left my seat and, pushing others aside, I rushed to the driver.

'*Alto, alto,*' I cried.

I was about to burst. Reluctantly the driver pulled over. I clambered from the bus and looked for a place to throw up. There was nothing, I had no choice. I dropped my pants and, squatting in full view of the bus load of Hondurans, I threw up and defecated at the same time. The driver tooted the horn impatiently. I cleaned myself with a clump of grass, then pulled up my pants and reboarded the bus, so weak I could hardly walk. No one smiled, they just stared, every eye fixed on me, disdainfully, as though I were a thing beneath contempt.

Sometimes life comes down to the rudiments. There is no choice but to go on, one's dignity totally crushed. I went to my seat, mortified, staring at each face individually, absorbing their disdain.

I spent the night in Tegucigalpa. By the morning the pain had subsided. There was nothing left inside me and the fever had gone. I decided to push on to Nicaragua.

At the bus station I went through the usual routine. Ask as many people as possible where the bus leaves from and when you get a consensus board that bus. Once on the bus, ask each passenger where they are going; if over half mention the name of your destination, then sit down, at least fifty percent sure you're on the right bus.

On the seat in front of me someone had written in big black letters 'Daniel 10, Yankis uno.' The pro-Sandinista quote turned my mind again to politics and the intrigues of travel. I wondered if it had been written by a Honduran or a Nicaraguan.

At the front of the bus a man peered around the edge of the door. Initially I could do nothing but stare as he eyed the passengers and then hauled himself up the stairs. I have seen a lot of disfigured bodies in my travels but this man was by far the worst. His face was horrifically scarred with what appeared to be leprosy. Below his shoulder, on the right side, was a large hump which extended all they way down his back. His pelvis rose and fell on alternate sides as he walked. Below the knees his legs were twisted so he could hardly stand. But, above all things, I remember the man's face as he waddled up the bus with his tray of fried bananas. Seldom have I seen such dignity as he offered his goods in turn to each person.

It brought back an image I had seen as a child, of Truganini, the last fullblooded Tasmanian Aboriginal. She had dignity. It came not from victory nor greatness; it came from resilience, the courage of being able to endure the worst that life could throw at her. As the man tapped my knee and held out his tray, I was overcome with mixed emotions; shame, guilt, relief, happiness; I could no longer differentiate between them.

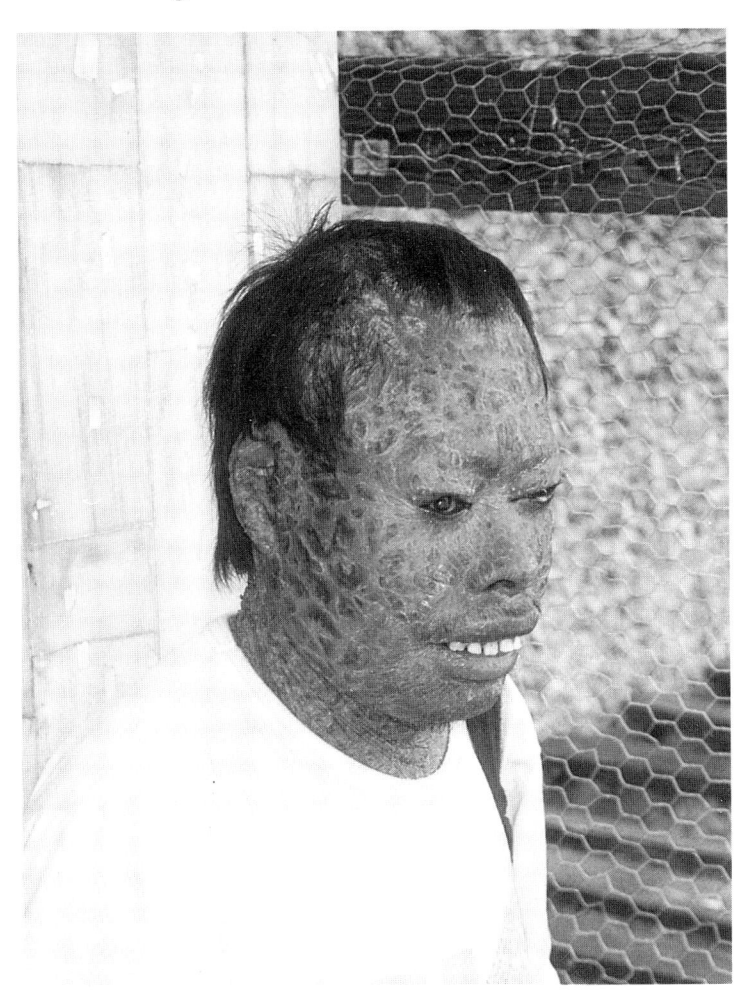

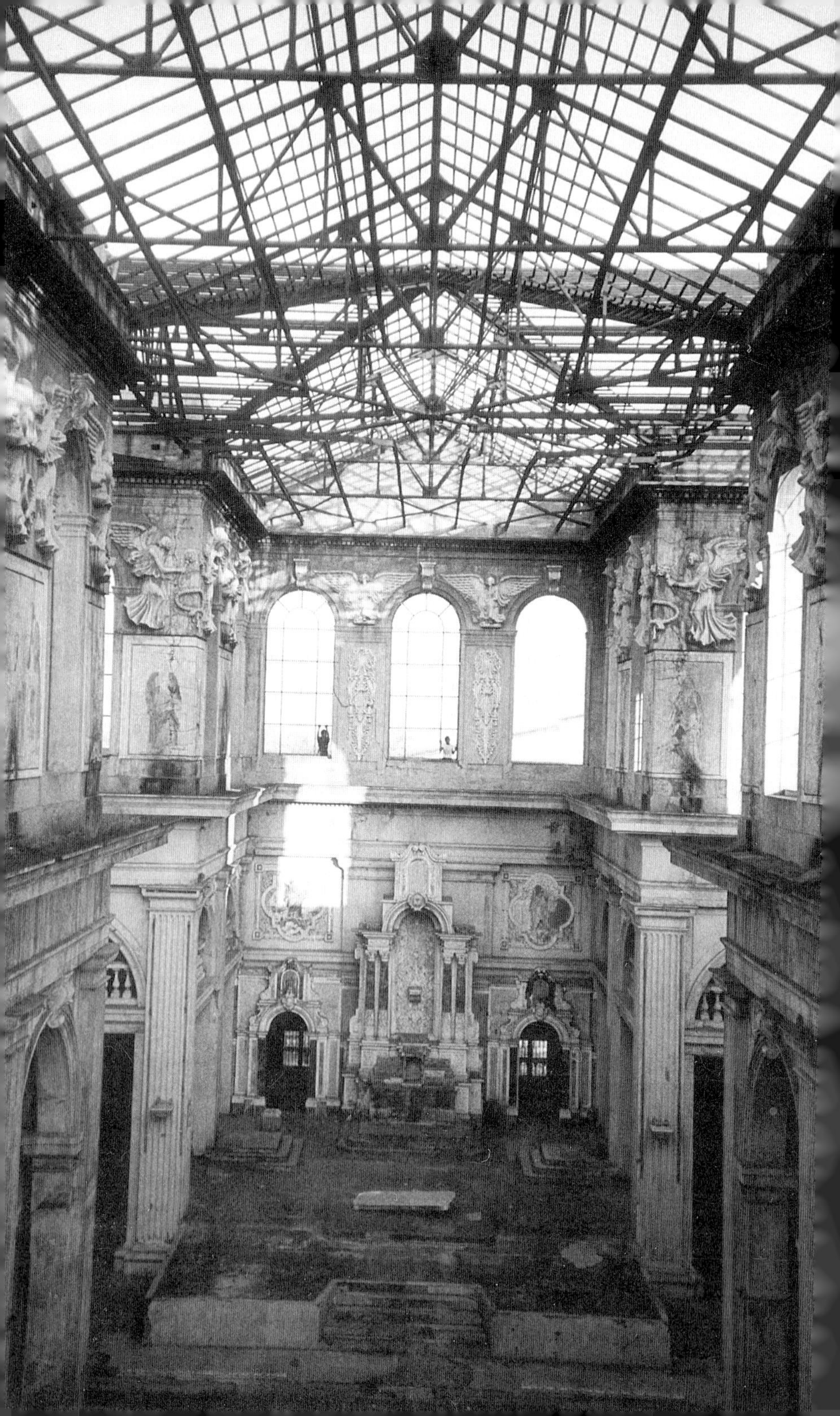

Nicaragua

MANAGUA is like a city that has just lost a prize fight. Punch-drunk and beaten by earthquakes and civil war, it can hardly stand. There are no substantial buildings, no typical Latin American bustle, the people are unfriendly and the city decaying and covered in graffitti.

On the bus driving in a man tried to rob me, but he was drunk and clumsy, so I hit him and called for help. Nobody on the bus moved as the driver pulled over and laconically threw us both off. I left my attacker lying on the grass and walked the rest of the way across town to the lake, where I had been told there was an old mission church. It was a hot day and except for a few cars, the streets were deserted.

When I arrived at the church, it too was empty, the earthquake having left little more than a facade of exposed rafters and glassless windows. The bell towers sat crooked upon their perches, cracked and ready to fall. Outside, a madman sat on the step, yelling and shaking his fist in the air at no one, his voice reverberating through the square.

The church wasn't ready to die: wind like warm breath blew through it off the lake, and bits of old roofing swung gently from the rafters and chattered in tongues on the floor. The vestry and baptismal areas were dark and smelled of urine. Voices whispered from upstairs. Apprehensively, I followed the voices up the staircase to where I found two men embracing by a windowsill. They kissed and ignored me as I passed. Below, some children had come to play and I found their laughter uncomfortably loud. Upstairs there were human faeces on the floor. I guessed people came here to sleep. The bell towers were pocked with bullet holes.

In the evening, however, I found a small, open-air cafe not far from my hostel, where I sat on the bamboo veranda, drank cold beer, and at last I felt relaxed.

'Do you mind if I join you?' said a voice from the table

behind. 'I can see you are alone and I too am alone so we should talk.'

I was glad of the company.

'My name is Chico,' said the man, who appeared in his mid-forties.

'I am eighteen years the head waiter at the Intercontinental Hotel,' he said, gesturing across the road to one of the few buildings still standing in Managua. 'I have dined with the Somozas, prepared banquets for the Ortegas.'

'Were you here during the earthquake?' I asked.

'I was right there,' he pointed to the hotel. 'It was terrible. Cracks so big you could put your arm down them, bodies everywhere. I saw at least sixty outside the cinema alone. I am a man,' said Chico, 'but that day I cried.'

'It must be difficult to live in a country with so much heartache.' I said.

Chico raised his eyebrows. 'I think no more difficult than anywhere else in the world. You foreigners tend to look too much at the whole picture and forget that it is just a reflection of a whole lot of little pictures. Nicaragua is no different to anywhere else. We are all in the middle. Someone is above you, someone below you. If you are a beggar or a banker it makes no difference.'

The man was drunk but I enjoyed his philosophy.

'For me, the Somoza regime was good,' he continued. 'He gave the best parties. I miss Somoza. For some, I know it was bad. But it's not politics. It's life. It is the same everywhere.'

When the bar closed we bought some more beer and went to Chico's room. The walls ware covered in posters of naked women, baseball cards and memorabilia from the hotel, including a picture of him with Somoza.

Chico slipped a cassette into his player. It was early Beatles' tunes recorded from a scratched record. He opened another beer.

'I am a man,' said Chico, 'but I cried the day John Lennon died.'

'Yeah I was upset too,' I said, remembering a hot Australian day when I first heard the news.

'You see,' said Chico, raising his beer, 'we are not so different, you and me.'

'Do you have family?' I asked.

'Three daughters and a wife,' said Chico proudly. 'The eldest is at university.'

'But you live here?' I said.

'I go home at weekends. Once I didn't go home for twenty-eight days. When I got home I said to my wife, 'Wife, are you mad?' She looked at me and said, 'Should I be?' I said, 'No,' and so she is not mad.'

Mosquitos buzzed around the dim light hanging from a cord on the roof while the life story of Desmond and Molly Jones played on the radio.

'The time I was away for twenty-eight days I took home four hundred dollars. I felt like a real man. I kept feeling the bulge of my wallet. When I arrived home my wife says I have to pay the rent. My eldest daughter needs money to pay her school fees. My youngest needs a new dress. The middle one has to go to the doctor. I drink a couple beers and I go to buy a shirt. In two days I have no money left. This is life, Jon,' said Chico, lying back on his bed. 'Someone is always above you, someone is always below you.'

'You are right Chico,' I said, finishing my beer. 'We are not so different, you and me.' But he hadn't heard me. He'd fallen asleep.

WARM, FIZZY DRINKS are the curse of all travellers and cold, fresh, clean, uncontaminated water the dream. It had been a hot day and I was contemplating my sixth bottle of Coke when I noticed a dour old man with a moustache selling fruit. I paid for three of his nicest-looking oranges and took them to the park across the street, sat down on a bench next to another man, and began to eat. The other man did not look up.

'Would you like some orange?' I said.

He turned around nervously and accepted. 'Thank you,' he said in broken English. 'I have not eaten for three days.'

The man did not look unhealthy and he was quite well dressed. His face however, was more rounded than was typical in Nicaragua, and his skin, much darker.

'Why?' I asked. He looked at me. I could see he was weighing up whether or not he could he trust me.

'I have escaped from prison,' he said, finally. I did not know what to reply.

'Why were you in prison?'

'I am a Moskite Indian,' he said. 'The Sandinista persecute us. I took revenge.'

From the little I knew about the Sandinista regime, what he had said may have been true. The Moskito Indians lived in relative isolation on the east coast, and had not fallen under the shadow of the Sandinista leader, Sandino, whose great black statue so dominated Managua and everything in it. They and other ethnic Indian minorities in the region considered themselves separate from the rest of Nicaragua. When the Sandinistas took over in 1979 they had tried to establish power in the region without taking into consideration the complexities of the social and religious circumstances. Backed by counter-revolutionaries and the United States, the Moskites mounted an attack which was soon quashed by the Sandinistas, who then forced them into relocation camps. Reports on the conditions of these camps vary, but it is not unreasonable to suppose this man may have suffered.

'What did you do?' I asked.

'What would you do if they killed your father for no reason?' I could not answer.

'I was in prison six years,' he said. 'Even the change of government did not help. They torture me many times. Look,' he said, lifting his shirt to reveal a small hole in his chest. 'Electric shock here and on my testicle.' He then pointed to his left eye. 'Cigarette ash,' he said. The eye was red and glazed. 'I am escaping to Costa Rica. My mother is there.'

I didn't know whether to believe the story or not. But the

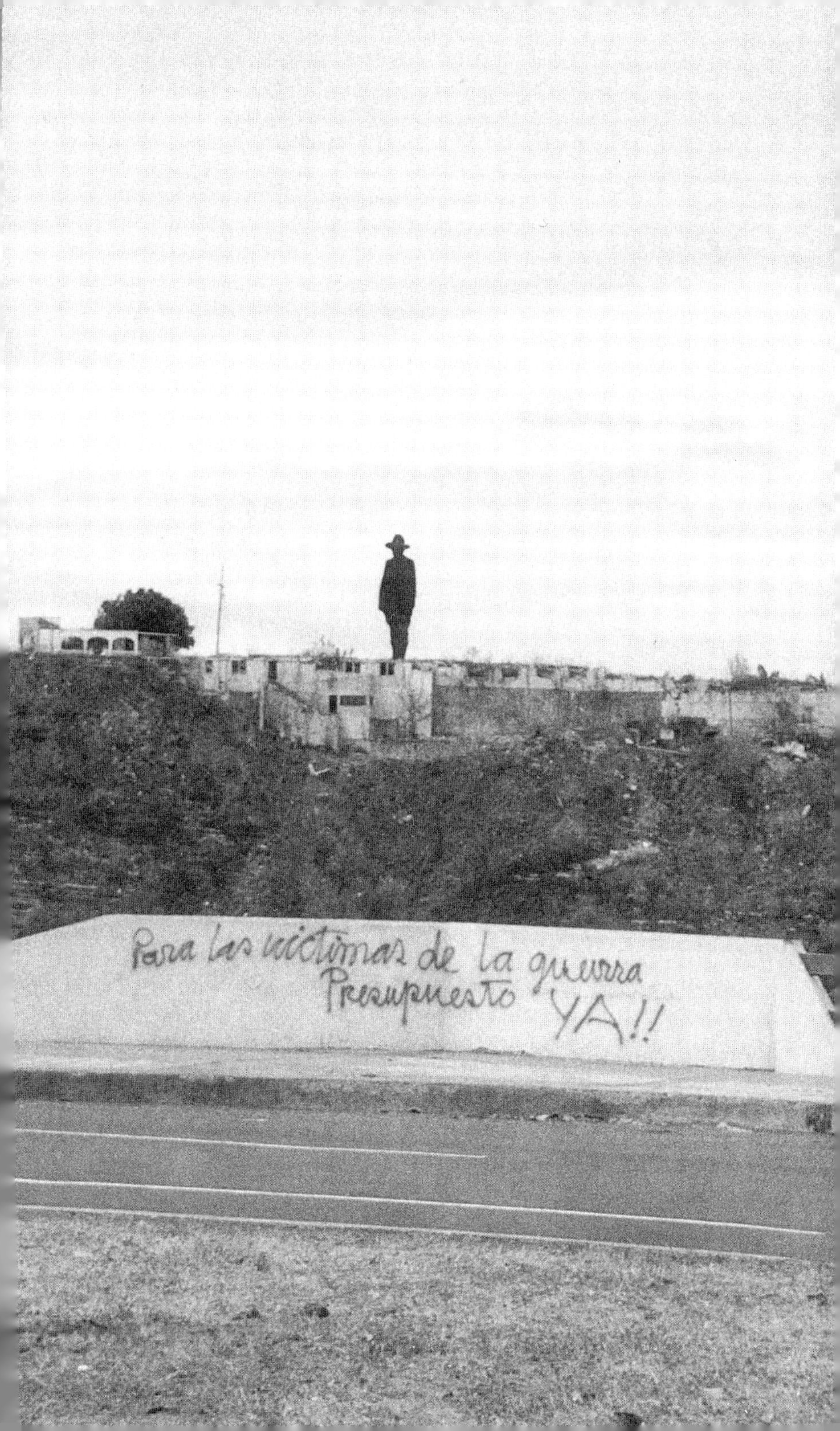
Para las victimas de la guerra
Presupuesto YA!!

man had asked for nothing so I sensed that what he said was true.

'How will you get there?' I asked.

'I must travel at night,' he said. 'Then I will cross the border in the jungle. It will take a week.'

'I am leaving for Costa Rica tomorrow on the bus,' I said. 'Would you like me to contact your mother when I arrive?'

'If you would do that, Jon, I would be indebted to you forever. I will write a letter and you could send it to her. Then if they catch me she will at least know I tried.'

I loaned him a pen and paper and he wrote the letter. When he had finished, he folded it and gave it to me.

'Now I must go,' he said. 'I can't sit in one place too long. I have no papers. If the police catch me I will go back to jail.'

'Look,' I said. 'Take this.' I gave him five dollars. 'I hope you make it.'

He took the five dollars and wrote my address on the back of his hand.

'When I reach Costa Rica I will send you back the money. You are a good person, Jon. Thank you.'

I have never heard from him. To this day I think of that man who, though he admitted to being a murderer, had seemed to deserve my help.

I sensed he was honest, but my traveller's instinct told me not to get involved; not to draw attention to myself and so I had given him only five dollars. Fifty dollars would have guaranteed him safe passage to Costa Rica. When I think of the power I had that day and how easily I avoided the responsibilities which went with it, I consider myself weak.

Four walls can be lonely. I had seen many in two years. Some wood, some brick, some clean, some not. I'd walk into a room, dump my pack, sit on the bed and watch my landlady close the door behind her. Suddenly time would stop. I'd swing my legs under the bed and look at the ceiling, check my watch. I'd wonder how long I could sleep to stave off the boredom, and I'd stare at a naked light bulb, wondering if it would light up when I turned it on.

I'd begin to hear myself move. The muffle of sheets as I turned on my bed, the tick of my watch, the clatter as I kicked off my shoes, the sound of my throat as I swallowed.

Outside there may be voices. They may be speaking in English or some language unknown, it doesn't matter, the happier they are, the lonelier I am. To force conversation is even lonelier. You can almost count the seven wonders of the world on one hand, but it's the time in between that is travelling. The Taj Mahal is beautiful but if it's 40°, your pack is heavy, your pockets have been picked and you have dysentery, you'd prefer the corner shop back home any day. You'd find a cool, shady spot and, on a marble step, bury your head in your hands and imagine you were lying in your bed back home and your Mum was bringing in a cool drink. You'd give anything to hear the sound of a magpie or the distant pock of cricket balls being hit in the park. Instead, a cockroach crawls from under your bed. It's shiny and black and it waves its little feelers around, then scuttles across the floor along the wall line and into a hole that isn't there. Muffled voices come through the walls or from the room above. Sometimes you hear lovers. The thought of reading or writing makes you sick so you lie and try to make out their words.

Sometimes you walk: in no particular direction, hands in pockets, looking more at your feet than at anything else. For kilometres you walk, thinking of a domestic scene in which you feel comfortable. You walk the streets of the world and think of home.

No matter how flexible you think you are, there are places where you just don't belong. When you close the door behind you, it's just you and four walls. Nobody else in the world knows you're in there. To have to rely solely on yourself to keep going. To be your own audience and your own companion is travel. It's not the Grand Canyon or the Taj Mahal, or Paris or Jerusalem; it's you alone with six billion people ... and four walls.

It takes time before you are immune to the tug of life. In the town of Esteli, a middle-aged man with a moustache and straw hat carried two armadillos home for lunch. Their feet were bound by pieces of string and their backs contorted at each attempt to free themselves. The clatter of their shells unsettled me, for like most Western people, I was not used to the sight of undomesticated animals being handled.

One of my most vivid childhood memories is of catching a fish with my uncle. Initially I had been excited by the tug on the other end of the line but as I reeled the fish in I became increasingly hesitant. Its delicate but desperate lunges vibrated up the rod and into my body, turning my stomach until eventually the thrashing silver fish broke the water and I dropped the rod in fright. My uncle picked up the rod, slung the fish on deck and I watched petrified while it flipped back and forth until it was exhausted.

'Take it off the hook,' my uncle ordered. I stared at the fish, captivated by the motion of its opening and closing mouth. Hesitantly I reached forward, drawing back each time the fish flipped.

'Go on,' taunted my uncle. 'Take the hook out.' I placed my hand over the fish, unable to pick it up, and felt the motion of its dying struggle. Weakly, I took the hook in my other hand and tried to free it.

'You've got to yank it,' my uncle said. I closed my eyes and yanked, pulling out half the fish's mouth as I did so. The fish began to bleed and I dropped it onto the deck where it lay, with its rounded eye staring up at me.

As I grew older, I had other similar experiences. I once went rabbit shooting with a friend on his farm and he shot a rabbit which managed to drag itself to a shallow hole before we reached it. My friend told me to pull it out. The rabbit was not yet dead and as I grabbed its trembling leg it kicked back, trying feebly to pull away. When the rabbit was out, my friend picked it up and twisted its neck like he was wringing out washing.

I have never been comfortable killing anything. He will take the animals home and kill them in mid-conversation with not a thought for their squeal or the warm blood that will spurt from their necks. His children will raise pigs or goats only to kill them and eat them.

TONIGHT I SLEEP in no-man's-land, trapped between the borders of Nicaragua and Costa Rica until the gates open in the morning. I am nowhere, but the prospect no longer daunts me. Nestled down, wrapped in plastic bags in the jungle, I feel my journey closing in around me. I think back two years, to when I left home and how at first I had tried so hard to fit in to places. I remembered the jewellery I had worn in Thailand, the things I had struggled to understand in Vietnam, my attempts to meet the people in Africa and the frustration I had felt when I realised the futility of trying.

I have travelled 80 000 kilometres through thirty-two countries and ended up in no country at all and I feel a strange relief; I think I am beginning to understand that in travel the only real boundaries are the ones we place around ourselves. This morning I took a photo of two machine guns hanging on the wall of the Nicaraguan border post. They were surrounded by number plates from all the different countries of Central America.

'What are the number plates?' I had asked the guard.

'They are the ones who didn't make it,' he chuckled.

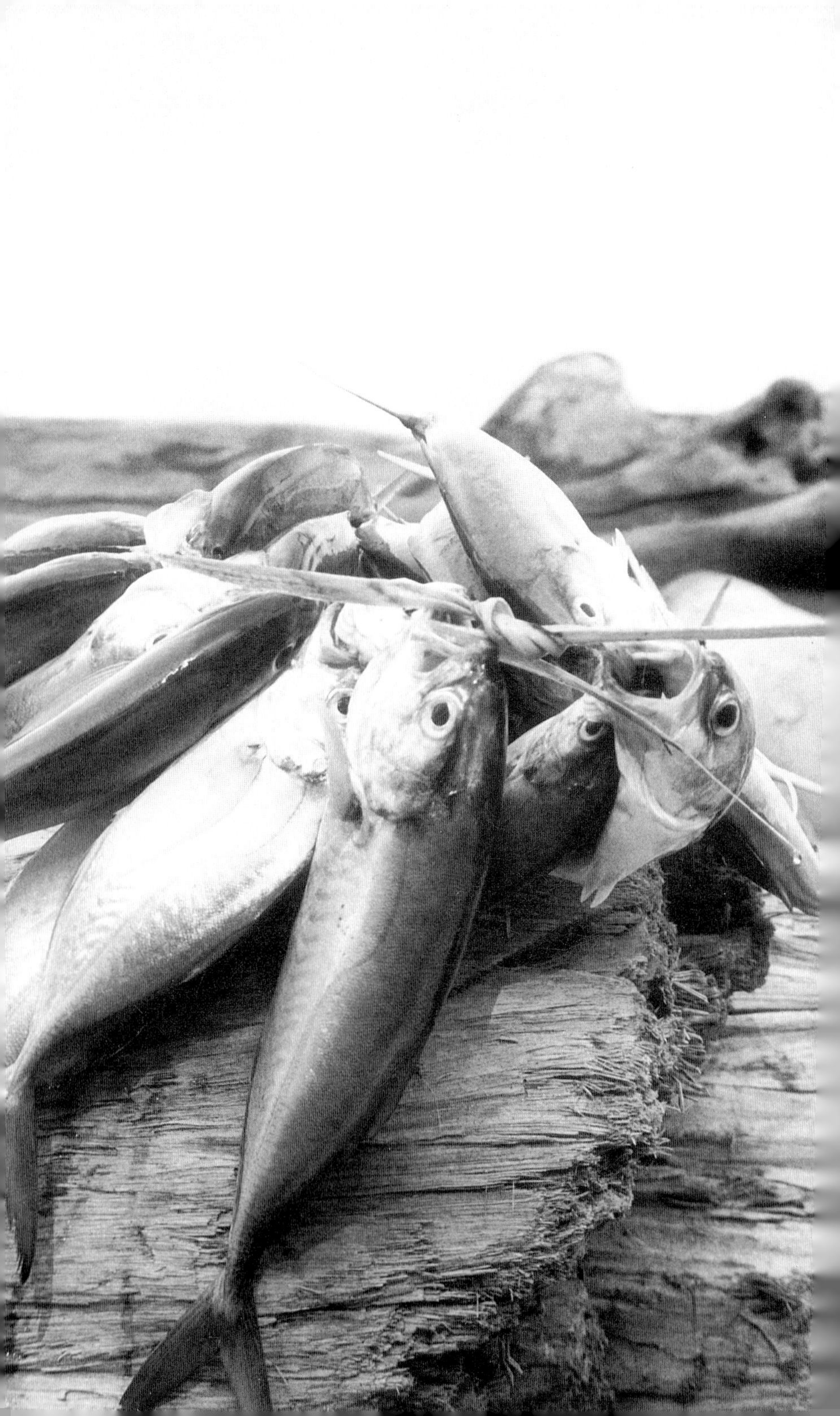

Costa Rica

EDUARDO SLAPPED THE FISH DOWN across a log. Moist silver scales glistened in the sunlight as the fish stared open-mouthed and wide-eyed into space. A piece of wire had been placed through their gills to carry them.

Eduardo turned to his boat, a small, wooden, dug-out canoe with an oar on either side. He began bailing water with an ice-cream container and I watched while the muscles in his shoulders and back rippled through his skin. Then he began to wind his lines around a piece of cork, methodically winding them back and forth in perfect lines. Next he put the cork inside a string bag and placed it into the bottom of his boat.

When he had finished, I moved forward from the jungle fringe where I had been observing.

'Good morning, Eduardo,' I said. 'You're up early.'

'I am always up early, like I told you in the bar last night, I am a fisherman,' he replied. I must catch twelve fish each day and everyone knows the best time to catch fish is the morning. So I am up early in the morning.'

'But we drank a lot last night,' I said, touching my head. 'You must be tired.'

'Yes,' said Eduardo. 'I am tired but I am also poor and so every day I must get up at five and catch twelve fish to sell to the restaurant. Every day for forty years I catch twelve fish.'

Eduardo hauled the boat out of the wash and onto the beach. He then stood back and looked at it.

'For forty years, I leave this boat on this beach,' he said. 'But for today I'm thinking to cover it in the jungle.'

'Why?' I asked.

'Two days ago one tourist stand in the bushes and take my photograph. This never happen in forty years. Today my swimming fins are stolen. This never happen for forty years either. One time one tourist asks for to borrow my boat. He give me twenty dollars but I tell him no. This boat is for fishing. He reads for me one book about a man and the sea and then he wants to be that man. But I tell him no. This book is for reading, this boat is for fishing. I can't read. He can't fish. So this tourist gets angry and he tells me this book won a big prize. But I tell him he wins this prize for writing, not for fishing and so he can't take my boat.'

'But twenty dollars is a lot of money, Eduardo. You would not have to work for a week.'

'But when this tourist sink this boat, then I don't work for a week also. And now I have no fins, I must hide this boat. For forty years my boat sits on the beach. Yesterday someone take my photograph, today someone take my fins, tomorrow someone steal my boat. No boat, no fins, no fish,' he said holding up the dozen he had left on the log.

We pulled the boat into the jungle and Eduardo covered it with leaves. When he had finished he turned to me, saying, 'Come, you can buy some beer and read to me some book in the sun,' he said. 'I like to listen to the tourists' stories; but please,' he continued, slinging the fish over his shoulder, 'Leave the fishing to me,'

THE DRIVE from San Jose to Cahuita had passed through the Costa Rican jungle, untouched, overgrown, with leaves as big as umbrellas coming right to the road. The abundant greenery was soothing after the sparsity of Nicaragua. At the highest point the bus had disappeared into the clouds and beads of water ran horizontally across the vibrating window. I had slept for most of the journey.

The morning before I was to return to Mexico, I sat on a log by the seaside. I was lonely, but also happy. When I travel with someone I allow them to entertain me and I grow lazy. Travelling alone enables you to look in places you might otherwise miss if you had company. It forces you to entertain yourself, to fill the long empty hours with observation.

I saw many things I would not have seen if I had had a companion: a rat building its nest; a bird, with its backside beating up and down, picking at bugs as it walked back and forth along the trunk of a fallen tree; a red balloon being tossed on the waves, fragile but unsinkable.

Further beyond, the sea rose and fell like the chest of a sleeping dog. Up and down in a slow smooth motion. Occasionally it exhaled onto the shore.

About a kilometre out, soundless white breakers rolled over the reef. Behind me the jungle was silent. It had rained during the night and on the surface of each leaf droplets still like insects. An ant scurried across the sand, as if aware it should not be out. Everywhere was a sleeping stillness.

The beach was empty. In the early morning I stripped to my trunks and walked towards the water, the crusty cool sand breaking beneath my feet. I began to breathe deeply the fresh jungle smells of moist leaves and wet wood. They filtered from my lungs into my chest, my arms, my legs and filled my body. Water ran beneath my feet, pulling me forward. I fixed my mask and snorkel. Deeper still, to my knees, my waist; I pushed forward from the bottom and filled my lungs, at first with short noisy breaths and then, gradually, with the motion of the sea.

I was weightless, stress flowed out of my body. I became the water. I abandoned myself, closed my eyes and drifted in the current, knowing always the reef was there, my protection, my ticket home.

Memories of my journey flowed in and out of my mind. I was at the foot of the Himalayas, the heart of Africa, sick again in India, alone in Nicaragua. They rolled into one, borne at random by the current. I was the sea, the moon, the earth, the stars; part of the universe; all of the universe. Sometimes there are no boundaries.

I wished now the reef was no longer there and that I could just drift like the red balloon. Miss Nga's words from Vietnam came back to me, 'I want to be like the water', she had said, 'I want to be like the water.' The words flowed between my bones and into my brain.

ON THE BUS BACK TO MEXICO I felt my trip begin to slip away from me. I tried to regain it, to draw it back, but I knew this time I would give in. Although my ticket did not expire for another month, I had run out of money and energy. I could think of nowhere in the world I would rather be than sitting beneath the liquidambar in my front yard at home, listening to the cricket on the ABC as it floated across the fence from next door. From that moment, my decision was made and the journey back to Mexico was a blur. I watched through the bus windows as men played large guitars; skinny dogs foraged in rubbish piles; trucks with bald tyres parked under Pepsi signs; men with machetes cut through banana trees; women with sacks walked on dusty roads; bare hills turned to lush jungle; children played in rivers; clothes dried on fences; a crowd stood around a dying dog which lifted its limp paw occasionally; oxen pulled wooden carts, their heads tied together on the yoke.

At the border between Guatemala and Mexico the connecting bus was not there. Nobody cared, they just said it would come. It did; sixteen hours late. I spent the time contemplating my return. I imagined the surprise on people's faces when, after two years, I walked back into their lives. I wondered how things had changed, if people had missed me or, as I suspected, if nothing had changed at all. It was scary at first to think that I would be returning with nothing tangible to show for my journey. My friends were all two years further on in their jobs, the girlfriend I had left at Melbourne airport was married and working in a new job, my footy team had played in its first finals series for years and were on the verge of breaking into the top league, a lot of my mates had married and were buying houses. I had known when I left home that things would not be the same when I returned, but it was only now that I was beginning to become apprehensive about it.

Returning to Mexico City was like meeting an old foe you once feared. This time it was challenging, but not intimidating. I would be there for just one day before I flew home.

It is ironic that Mexico should be my final destination. Once when I was still at school, I had sat in the back of a maths class with a friend and planned a trip to Mexico. Why we chose Mexico I don't know. I think it was something to do with the sounds of the names. Between us we knew nothing of its past or present culture. We just wanted to go to Mexico.

As the bus entered the city limits I knew what to expect. I knew the roads and the people, the hotels and the shops. I knew some of the history, of how the new Mexico City was built on top of the old, of how one culture obliterated another, how there bubbles beneath the surface – the tortured souls of Aztec warriors rising and losing direction, watered down in the cesspool of the uncertain interracial mixes that exist today. But I only 'know' it because I read it. I never really understood it; saw it with my own eyes or felt it in my heart. The truth is I don't know Mexico City at all. I had travelled for over two years and at my final destination, I was still ignorant.

EPILOGUE

The full moon cast a silver spot on the aircraft wing. The sky was an endless, dark greyish-blue. One star shone above cotton clouds lolling, white and grey, across the horizon. The plane seemed stationary, trapped in time and space, rocking gently. I was in the bosom of the universe, going home.

We flew through two days in twenty-eight hours. Five countries, two continents; fixed, but lost in time and space. The world was enormous and yet just a dot, unlit and smaller than that lone star. I had flown half way around it in a day and yet barely touched it in two-and-a-half years. But travel is not so much about going as it is about leaving; it is not so much about seeing the world, as seeing yourself in it.

The lolling clouds clumped into cauliflowers as dawn broke under the sky. We began our descent into Melbourne, where my family was waiting, watching the sinking plane, with me in it, waiting to touch down.